In memory of Peter Letchford, beloved husband, father, grandfather, missionary, pastor, leader, and happy servant of God.

Smile!

God Loves You

Smile!

God Loves You!

A collection of Christmas
messages and sermon
illustrations by Peter Letchford

Compiled by
Jessica Gierlichs
(née Letchford)

Optasia Books
PO Box 2011
Friendswood, Texas 77549

Dedication

To Gramps
Who always had a wise and
witty answer to our questions.

We love you and miss you.

A Note from Dorothy Letchford

When she was a student at Yale University, Jessica, our first grandchild, was a frequent visitor in our home during school breaks because her parents, Dr. Steve and Dr. Sherri Letchford, were missionaries in Africa. She was curious about our backgrounds so not only asked us questions but would peruse scrapbooks or articles that answered some of these.

So it was not surprising, when Jessica was visiting me after Peter had died the previous December, that she busied herself at the computer in our office tidying up our files. She is much more adept at this sort of thing than I am, so I was extremely grateful for her help and let her carry on without making any inquiries.

The following Christmas, I opened a package from Jessica and found 3 copies of this book. She had compiled stories and illustrations told by my dear husband, Peter, from his computer when she was working in our office. I was surprised beyond measure and treasure this printed reminder of my gifted husband--who was able to help his listeners apply scripture to everyday life in a memorable way.

Table of Contents

Part 1
CHRISTMAS STORIES

As told at Christmas Eve Services

NO ROOM IN THE INN— BEGONE!

Boys and girls, back when your moms and dads were boys and girls I told them a story about a place called Centerville, where they put on a Christmas Pageant every year on December 24.

It was, of course, all about the birth of Jesus in Bethlehem, and the whole town took part in it.

Well, one year they decided that next year's pageant was going to be the greatest ever. And it needed to be, because the previous year the pageant had been a bit of a disaster.

First of all, the real, live donkey that was carrying Mary onstage, with Joseph walking right behind it, got scared when he saw all the people staring at him, and stopped and refused to move another inch. Which of course brought the pageant to a complete halt.

Then there was a problem with one of the angels.

The angels, who were all Centerville 4th graders, had to float across the stage, suspended on a wire and singing Gloria in Excelsis Deo, "glory to God in the highest."

Well, the problem was that one of these temporary angels didn't fasten her belt tight enough, and halfway across the stage it came undone and she fell on top of the two shepherds who were leading two live sheep into the stable.

She did not damage the sheep, but the two shepherds needed quite a bit of first aid, one having a broken nose and the other a black eye.

So preparations for the next year started eleven months in advance, and, like I said, they were determined it would be the best one ever.

The actors, as usual, where all townspeople, chosen by a committee. But there was one man in the town who had never been chosen and, frankly, was not likely ever to be chosen.

His name was Willy. I guess he had a last name, but no one ever used it. To everyone in Centerville, he was just Willy.

Willy weighed 300 pounds, and he was one of those guys who moved slow, spoke slow, thought slow, worked slow. The committee could not think of any part in the play that he would be suitable for.

Ah, but Willy also had a nice smile for everyone. He was a happy sort of guy, and everyone sort of liked him, Yes, and they felt sorry for him too.

You see, years before, when Willy was a young man, and neither fat nor slow, he had married the sweetest, prettiest girl in town, but she had died having a baby ten months after their wedding. And the day she died, if you can believe it, was Christmas Eve, the same day on which the pageant was held each year.

Anyway, after his wife and baby died, Willy stopped going to church, and he started drinking too much liquor. And that's how he came to get fat and slow, and more and more unsuitable for a part in the pageant.

He moved into a cheap one-room apartment at the edge of town. Actually, it was a big old farmhouse which someone had turned into one-room apartments, but when Willy had applied for one, they told him they had all been taken.

But the owner said there was a place outside in the yard, which had been an old cowshed, and if Willy wanted to fix it up, he could have it.

So Willy took it, and despite his troubles, he kept his smile.

And that smile, plus people feeling sorry for him because, years ago, he had lost his wife and baby on Christmas Eve, made everyone want him to have a part in the next pageant.

So the committee said OK, he could be the innkeeper, because he would then have only one line to say, which was: "No room at the Inn! Begone!"

Well, I can't tell you how excited Willy was. He had eleven months to learn that one line, and he got started on it on right away.

In due course, Christmas Eve arrived again. The weather for the Pageant was good and the crowds fantastic.

Somehow they managed to get 300-pound Willy into the Inn they had made mostly of cardboard, and the moment came when Joseph walked onstage, leading the donkey (a well-behaved one this year) with Mary on its back.

Joseph knocked at the door of the cardboard Inn, and the door opened, and Willy managed to squeeze through it without knocking the whole place down.

Everyone was breathless, as Joseph said, "Please sir, find us a room in your Inn if you can. We have come a long way, and my wife is very tired."

This was Willy's great moment. He filled his lungs with air, and in a slow but booming voice he said, "No room in the Inn. Begone!"

With a sad face, Joseph started to move away, but before he had gone far, he thought he would give it a second shot, and turned back.

The Innkeeper was still standing there. And Joseph, in a really pleading voice, said "O sir, please see if you can find us even a small room, even if it is only a cowshed out in your backyard. You see, my wife is pregnant, and it looks like the baby may come this very night. She really needs somewhere to rest, or she may die and the baby too."

That really quietened Willy down, but he knew he had to say his line, so in not much more than a whisper he said, "No room in the Inn. Begone."

So once again Joseph turned to leave.

But then tears started rolling down Willy's face. He thought of that Christmas Eve years before, when he had looked down on his sweet wife and their baby, both dead.

And as Joseph neared the edge of the stage, leading the donkey and Mary on it, Willy filled his lungs with air once again, and boomed out these words:

"Jo! Jo! Come back. Jo, come back. You can have my room. It's in the backyard of the Apartments, in fact, it used to be a cowshed, but you can have it! And there's room for the donkey in there too!"

OK, kids. Now do you think that is a true story or not?

Well, I don't think it matters much whether it is or whether it isn't. For they say that, from that point on, Willy was a completely different man.

It wasn't just that he started going to church again, but he stopped drinking large quantities of liquor, and

18

thus trimmed his weight down to a reasonable size, and he started talking to people as well as smiling at them.

And at the plant where he worked, they say he started talking to people about Jesus.

And when they asked him what had made him suddenly start telling everybody about Jesus, he said that, "Oh, it was right there in the pageant. I knew that, if I kept Joseph and Mary out, I would be keeping the baby Jesus out. And I just could not go on saying to Jesus, "I've got no room for you. Begone!" So I let Him in."

Boys and Girls, yes, and moms and dads, if you'd been the Innkeeper in the play, you would have said the same, wouldn't you?

You would have stopped saying "No" to Jesus, and asked Him to come into your heart.

THE TABLECLOTH

The brand-new pastor and his wife, newly assigned to their first ministry - to reopen a church in suburban Brooklyn, arrived in early October, excited about their opportunities. When they saw their church, it was very rundown and needed much work. They set a goal to have everything done in time to have their first service on Christmas Eve.

They worked hard, repairing pews, plastering walls, painting, and on December 18 were ahead of schedule and just about finished. On December 19, a terrible tempest – a driving rainstorm – hit the area and lasted for two days.

On December 21, the pastor went over to the church. His heart sank when he saw that the roof had leaked, causing a large area of plaster about 20 feet by 8 feet to fall off the front of the sanctuary just behind the pulpit, beginning about head-high. The pastor cleaned up the mess on the floor, and not knowing what else to do but postpone the Christmas Eve service, headed home. On the way he noticed that a local business was having a flea market sale for charity, so he stopped in. One of the items was a beautiful, handmade, ivory-coloured crocheted tablecloth with exquisite work, fine colours and a Cross embroidered right in the centre. It was just the right size to cover up the hole in the front wall. He bought it and headed back to the church.

By this time, it had started to snow. An older woman running from the opposite direction was trying to catch the bus. She missed it. The pastor invited her to wait in the warm church for the next bus 45 minutes later. She sat in a pew and paid no attention to the pastor while he got a ladder, hangers, etc., to put up the tablecloth as a wall tapestry.

The pastor could hardly believe how beautiful it looked – it covered up the entire problem area.

Then he noticed the woman walking down the centre aisle. Her face was like a sheet. "Pastor," she asked, "where did you get that tablecloth?"

The pastor explained. The woman asked him to check the lower right corner to see if the initials EBG were crocheted into it there. They were. These were the initials of the woman, and she had made this tablecloth thirty-five years before, in Austria.

The woman could hardly believe it as the pastor told how he had just gotten the tablecloth. The woman explained that before the war, she and her husband were well-to-do people in Austria.

When the Nazis came, she was forced to leave. Her husband was going to follow her the next week.

She was captured, sent to prison and never saw her husband or her home again. The pastor wanted to give her the tablecloth; but she made the pastor keep it for the church. The pastor insisted on driving her home, that was the least he could do. She lived on the other side of Staten Island and was only in Brooklyn for the day for a housecleaning job.

What a wonderful service they had Christmas Eve. The church was almost full. The music and the spirit were great. At the end of the service, the pastor and his wife greeted everyone at the door and many said that they would return.

One older man, whom the pastor recognized from the neighbourhood, continued to sit in one of the pews and stare, and the pastor wondered why he wasn't leaving. The man asked him where he got the tablecloth on the front wall, because it was identical to one that his wife had made years ago when they lived in Austria before the war and how could there be two tablecloths so much alike? He told the pastor how the Nazis came, how he forced his wife to flee for her safety, and he was supposed to follow her, but he was arrested and put in a prison. He never saw his wife or his home again all the thirty-five years in between.

The pastor asked him if he would allow him to take him for a little ride. They drove to Staten Island and to the same house where the pastor had taken the woman three days earlier. He helped the man climb the three flights of stairs to the woman's apartment, knocked on the door and he saw the greatest Christmas reunion he could ever imagine.

GOOD, BETTER, BEST

This isn't really a Christmas homily, because it's about some people in the Old Testament and so it all happened way back before Christmas ever started.

But it is a story about a young couple who lived in Bethlehem, and their names were . . . oh man, what *were* their names?

Anyway, their names were not Joseph and Mary, because like I said they're in the Old Testament not the New.

But they were young Mr. Somebody and young Miss Somebody, and at about fifteen years of age, they fell in love and got married.

And don't let that put ideas into your heads, you 15-year-olds. You can do all sorts of things if you are somebody in the Old Testament that you can't do if you are just somebody in Augusta.

Anyway, this young couple got married and within a year they had received from God a most wonderful gift: a baby boy. Man, did they ever whoop it up and shout "Hallelujah, it's a boy!"

But then, you see, the same thing happened the next year, except they had a girl.

So once again they whooped it up and shouted, "Hallelujah, now we have one of each."

But now something happened which you will hardly believe, and frankly I wouldn't believe it if it wasn't in the Bible. I'm certain it never happened in your family and I know it never did in mine.

What happened was that they went on having babies, one every year, until finally they thirty sons and thirty daughters – sixty kids. It could be they had lots of twins and triplets, possibly even quadruplets, or quintuplets. The Bible doesn't tell us.

All I know is that they had thirty sons and thirty daughters, and if you don't believe me you can read about it for yourself in Judges 12:8-10, where it says: "Ibzan of Bethlehem" – ah, that was his name, and his wife's name was Mrs Ibzan, anyway, Ibzan served as Judge in Israel. He had thirty sons and thirty daughters, and when they grew up he sent his daughters abroad to find husbands, and then brought in thirty daughters-in-law from abroad for his sons. Which means that before long they must have had about 300 grandchildren.

OK, you may say, but what's that got to do with Christmas?

Well, "Nothing much," I guess. It's just that some years ago I did the wedding of a young couple, and when I came to that bit where I say, "Who gives this woman to be married to this man?," and the girl's father has to say "I do," or "Her mother and I do," this girl's father could hardly get the words out because he started to cry.

He was giving away his only daughter.

And now here was this guy Ibzan of Bethlehem giving away thirty daughters!

Look, I know you can stretch these Bible stories to mean all sorts of things that they don't really mean, but as I think what it must have cost Ibzan to send half his family away, I think of that first Christmas when God gave away His whole family.

For God only had one Son, and that was Jesus, and it seems like one day He must have said, "Son, we've got it so good up here in heaven, everything is perfect, but that poor old world down there is in one awful mess. The people are cussing and swearing, and lying and thieving, and shooting and killing. Would you please go down and tell them I still love them, and I am ready to forgive them, and I'll do everything that's needed for them to get their sins forgiven and stop them being wicked and start being like you, my only begotten Son?"

"Son, would you do that for Me? They probably will not like you. They may even kill you. But will you go?"

So God sent his son away from home, which was heaven, and he came all the way down here to earth. He's God's great Christmas gift to us.

But it's like it is with all our Christmas gifts, they are not really ours until we take them, and say "Thank You" for them.

Just remember Christmas Day is the day when God gave us the best gift he could ever have given us, all wrapped up in baby clothes, and placed where we could easily find him, in a manger, right there in Bethlehem where Ibzan lived.

So be sure to say "Thank You" to God and tell him that you wouldn't trade his gift of Jesus for all the other gifts you have received or will ever receive at Christmas.

THE BEST CHRISTMAS PAGEANT EVER

Clark has rightly forbidden me to preach to you this evening.

I am simply to tell you a Christmas story. Now there are two sorts of Christmas stories. There are the Biblical ones, with which I am sure you are all familiar. Then there are the fictional stories, of which I know three, and of which I will tell you one.

And I apologize in advance that it is one you probably know already. I got this story from a book called *The Best Christmas Pageant Ever*. And on the back of the book there was a note saying that it was now America's favourite Christmas Story. So most likely a good many of you will know the story already, and if this is so, please listen carefully and see if I make any changes, or, as I would call them, "improvements."

It's all about these six Herdman kids, Ralph, Imogene, Leroy, Claude, Ollie and Gladys. Six skinny, string-haired kids, all alike except for being different ages and sizes. They were absolutely the worst kids in the history of the world. They lied and stole and smoked cigars (and that included the girls) and talked dirty and hit little kids and cussed their teachers and took the name of the Lord in vain and set fire to Fred Shoemaker's old broken-down tool house.

They even had a mad cat. It had one short leg and a broken tail and one missing eye, and the mailman wouldn't deliver anything to the Herdmans' house because of it. One day Claude Herdman took this cat to school for Show and Tell. He hadn't fed it for three days so it was already mad, but then he carried it to school in a box, and when he opened the box, the cat shot out straight up in the air, and then tore around all over the place, scratching little kids, shedding fur, scattering books and finally bringing down the aquarium full of twenty gallons of water and about sixty-five goldfish. It finally settled down a bit, but only because it was busy eating the sixty-five gold fish plus two pet mice that one of the kids had brought to "Show and Tell."

Now in this small town where the Herdmans lived, there was a small church which put on a Christmas pageant every year. It wasn't what you would call 4-star entertainment. The script was standard (I mean there was the inn, the stable, the shepherds, the star, and so on). The primary school kids were the angels, and the intermediates, the shepherds. And finally six kids had to be found to be Joseph, Mary, the three Wise Men and the Angel of the Lord.

Now this pageant had been going on for so many years that the kids in the church found it boring, and had to be more or less conscripted to take part in it. Thus the biggest boys were automatically the Wise Men, and Elmer Hopkins, the pastor's son, was always Joseph, and had been as long as anyone could remember. Of course nobody ever thought about the Herdman kids in connection with the pageant. They didn't even come to church.

But this particular year it so happened that Leroy Herdman, on one of those rare days when he decided to go to school, sat next to a nice kid named Charlie Robinson, who let it slip out that once again he was going to have to be one of the shepherds who watched their flocks by night in the church pageant.

"What's a pageant?" Leroy asked.

"It's a sort of play," said Charlie.

"Then I'm coming," said Leroy, "I love the movies."

And come he did – to that first rehearsal.

In fact, all six of the Herdman kids came, and you should have heard what some of the church people had to say about that.

Some even thought the pastor should be fired for letting them in, even though he hadn't even known they were coming. Some even said they'd never come to that church again.

But there the Herdman kids were at that first rehearsal.

"What's the play all about?" one of them asked Charlie.

"It's about Jesus," Charlie said.

"Everything around here seems to be about Jesus," said the Herdman kid.

Anyway, the older boys and girls were duly conscripted to be shepherds and guests at the inn and so on, and "All we need now," said Charlie's mother, who was leading the rehearsal, "is a Mary and a Joseph, and three Wise Men and the Angel of the Lord."

Charlie's mother then explained about what sort of girl Mary needed to be.

"We all know what kind of person the real Mary was," she said. "She was quiet and gentle and kind, and the girl who plays Mary should try to be that sort of person. I know that many of you would like to be Mary in our pageant, but we can only have one Mary so I'll ask for volunteers."

Well, the only girl to put up her hand was Imogene Herdman.

"I want to be Mary," she said, and then, looking back over her shoulder, she added, "and my brother Ralph wants to be Joseph."

"Yeh," Ralph said.

Charlie's mother just stared at them.

"Well," she said after a minute, "we want to be sure that everyone has a chance, don't we? Does anyone else want to volunteer to be Joseph or Mary?"

No one did.

No one ever did, especially not Elmer Hopkins, the pastor's son.

"All right," Charlie's mother said, "Ralph will be our Joseph and Imogene will be Mary."

And since no one else volunteered to be the Wise Men, Leroy, Claude and Ollie Herdman were appointed.

There was one Herdman left over and one main role left to be filled, namely the Angel of the Lord, so, of course, Gladys Herdman got that part.

Well, when the news of that got out, needless to say Charlie's mother's phone started to ring off the hook. Mrs. Hazelbeck, for example, asked quite angrily if it was true that Imogene Herdman was going to be Mary the mother of Jesus in the church play.

"Yes," she said, "Imogene is going to be Mary."

"And the rest of the Herdmans are going to be in it too?" the lady asked.

"Yes," replied Charlie's mother, "Ralph is going to be Joseph and the others are the Wise Men and the Angel of the Lord."

"You must be crazy!" said the woman at the other end of the line; "I live next door to that bunch with their yelling and screaming and their insane cat and their garage door going up and down, up and down all day long. The whole idea is disgraceful."

Charlie's mother got lots of other telephone calls, most of them real nasty, but all that did was make her determined to make that year's pageant the very best Christmas pageant anyone ever saw, and to do it with the Herdmans too.

"After all," she said to her husband, "they raised their hands and nobody else did and that's that."

And it was, too. For one thing, if Charlie's mother resigned, nobody else wanted to take over the pageant with or without the Herdmans. And for another thing, Pastor Hopkins got so fed up with all the complaints that he was pretty well telling everybody to go jump in the lake, or at least reminding them that when Jesus said, "Suffer the little children to come to me," he meant all the little children, including the Herdmans. Finally the telephone callers gave up and the rehearsals continued on the following Wednesday.

The Herdman kids got there ten minutes late, sliding into the room like a bunch of outlaws about to shoot up a saloon. Charlie's mother started to separate out the angels and the shepherds and the guests at the inn, and at once Claude Herdman demanded to know what an Inn was.

"It's like a motel," somebody told him, "where people spend the night."

"You mean Jesus spent the night in a motel?" said Claude.

"No," said Charlie's mother. "Jesus wasn't even born yet. It was Mary and Joseph who wanted to stay there, but there was no vacancy so the owner told them to go and sleep out in the cowshed."

Then Leroy Herdman wanted to know why someone hadn't knocked that motel keeper flat on the ground for refusing a room in the main building and putting them out in a shed.

And Ollie Herdman wanted to know if a manger was some sort of bed, and why would they have a bed in a cowshed.

When she was told that a manger was not a bed, but a food trough, and they put the baby Jesus in that because they had to put the baby somewhere.

"Yeh," she said, "that's like it was when our Gladys was born. We were out of beds and had to put her in a dresser drawer."

"Aw, shut up," yelled Imogene Herdman to her siblings, and then turned to Charlie's mother and demanded that she begin at the beginning, and tell them exactly what happened at that first Christmas.

So she picked up her Bible and read the Christmas story, with each one of the Herdman kids, famous for never sitting still and never paying attention to anyone, staring at her and drinking in every word, while most of the church kids fidgeted and fussed because they'd heard it dozens of times before and knew it backwards and forwards.

And as they drank that story in, the Herdman kids started to get angry, first with the Innkeeper, then with the Three Kings because of the junky gifts they brought, stupid things like frankincense and myrrh which no one had ever heard of.

Three Kings? Three phonies so far as the Herdmans were concerned, who should have been shot as Herod's spies.

But it was Herod himself they got most angry about, figuring the FBI should have investigated him and shot him as a terrorist.

And by the time that rehearsal was over, the six Herdman kids were solidly on the side of the Baby Jesus. Their only regret was that they had not been around there in Bethlehem at the time. They would have taken care of the situation in short order.

So rehearsal followed rehearsal, and finally the only thing left was for Charlie's mother to find an actual baby who could be Jesus.

This had never been a problem in previous years, but this year, when mothers found out that the Herdmans were involved, they withdrew their offers.

But this did not worry Imogene a bit. "I'll get us a baby," she said.

"How would you do that?" Charlie's mother asked.

"Easy," said Imogene. "There's always two or three babies in carriages outside the supermarket. I'll take one."

Needless to say, Charlie's mother vetoed that idea, but that did not worry Imogene.

"OK, I'll get me a baby doll, which will be better anyway. Baby dolls don't mess their pants."

And that's how it was the night of the pageant. The church kids, who knew the Christmas story backwards and forwards, were backstage, and the six Herdman kids who'd never been to church before were front stage.

And in the final scene, when everyone – angels, shepherds, wise men, the whole lot – were gathered around the Baby Jesus in the manger, singing "O come let us adore him, Christ the Lord," all eyes turned on Imogene.

She was weeping, and great big tears were making great big streaks down her unwashed face, and the other five Herdman kids were standing there staring at her and the baby Jesus as though it was the most wonderful thing they had seen in their whole lives.

I can't go beyond that, because that's where the book in which I read this story ends, but I'm going to make a guess.

I believe that, as they stared at that baby doll in that cardboard manger, those Herdman kids began to see what those verses that Charlie's mother had read to them from the Bible were all about, verses like "His name Jesus means he can save us from our sins" or that verse which says that Jesus is "God is with Us."

I'm not saying that they all suddenly became Christians, but I am saying that it would be mighty strange, wouldn't it, if you and I, we who know the whole story backwards and forwards, are hardly moved at all by it towards loving and trusting Jesus, when those six scruffy, skinny, string-haired Herdman kids were moved to tears by it?

I'm asking *you*, that would be real strange, wouldn't it?

FRED

I've run out of fictional Christmas stories after all these years, so let me tell you a true one instead. I've written it out because Clark has told me that you will not be in any mood to sit through one of those long-winded sermons we preachers make you sit through on Sundays.

It's about my old friend Fred Stuto. The facts are true as far as I can remember them, and where I can't remember them, I've made them up.

Fred was an alcoholic, whose wife had finally walked out on him because of his brutality.

She had taken their three younger children with her, leaving their oldest, a 16-year-old boy with him.

His next-door neighbour was a widow who attended the church I was pastoring in upstate New York. One evening about a month before Christmas, she called me to relate that Fred, drunk as usual, had half-strangled his teenage son and had come to her for help.

Could she bring him over to me?

So over they came, Fred still half-drunk, and scared out of his wits, thinking he had probably murdered his son. And after the manner of intoxicated people, he wept and moaned, and promised to turn his life over to Jesus that very moment.

I told him not to rush it, but to come back the next day when he was sober, and able to make a real decision: which he did. He was very soundly converted to Christ, or to use the phrase popularized by Jimmy Carter, was "born again," and with his new birth came new life.

And that new life was so spectacularly different from his old life that as the weeks went by, it became a talking point amongst all his relatives and his wife's relatives.

"Fred's really got religion," they said.

Fred's wife wasn't greatly impressed.

After all, that's what liquor does to people. It makes them so they can repent with tears one day, and go off and get blind drunk the next.

But it got to be Christmas Eve.

His wife in the meantime had become a Christian, and even though she did not really believe all the things she was hearing about Fred, she felt the Lord was telling her to send him word that he could come by her house, and she would open the door just a chink, just to see if he looked any different.

So he went and knocked at her door, and she opened it a chink, then flung the door wide open and fell into his arms.

He was different all right. Clean and smart and with that same twinkle of love in his eyes that he'd had on their wedding day.

And the next day was Christmas, and it was as though "to them a child had been born and a son been given; and from then on the government was going to be upon his shoulder, and his name for them would be Wonderful Counselor, Mighty God, Everlasting Father, Prince of Peace" (Isaiah 9:6).

Of course there is nothing unique in this story. The same thing has happened many times before and since, including in the Bible.

Mark 5:1-19 tells how one day Jesus was accosted by a deranged and very violent man who lived in the tombs in the graveyard. He was so violent that, when they bound him with shackles and chains, he wrenched the chains apart, and he broke the shackles in pieces.

No one had the strength to subdue him.

Night and day among the tombs and on the mountains he was always crying out and bruising himself with stones.

But one day he saw Jesus from afar, he ran and fell down before him. And Jesus said, "Come out of the man, you unclean spirit!"

Now a great herd of pigs was feeding there on the hillside, and the spirits came out, and entered the pigs, and the herd, numbering about 2,000, rushed down the steep bank into the sea and drowned.

The herdsmen fled and told it in the city and in the country. And people came to see what it was that had happened. And they saw the demon possessed man, sitting there, clothed and in his right mind.

And he begged Jesus that he might go with him, but Jesus said "No. Go home to your friends and tell them how much the Lord has done for you, and how he has had mercy on you. Tell them how I first *emptied* you of the demons, and then filled you with Myself – filled you with all the fullness of God."

Can you imagine what happened when the man arrived back home?

OK, so it was not Christmas Day, but it was a great day anyway.

The man's frightened wife had probably boarded up the windows and bolted the doors, and forbidden the children to let anyone into the home.

But then came this knock at the door, and one of the kids could not resist the temptation to see who it was.

"It's daddy! He's come back! But he's so different!"

Finally the frail mother opens the door a chink, and standing there is the handsome man she had married, now washed, shaved, dressed, composed, and with the same love in his eyes that he'd had on their wedding day.

She gazes at him for a moment and then, all fear gone, she flings open the door and leaps into his arms – into the arms of a man Created Anew in Jesus Christ, created in Him unto good, kindly, loving works, which God had before ordained that he should walk in them: a man now well on the way to bearing the Image and the Likeness of his Saviour and God.

What is there in Christmas that is better than that?

Christmas is Christ coming into The World.

But that story is Christ coming into Your World and My World, delivering us from evil, saving us from sin, and launching us into the sort of life that makes the angels sing, "Glory to God in the Highest."

Part 2
Sermon Illustrations

SIR STEWART GORE-BROWNE'S RECEPTION OF MY AFRICAN TEAM

I remember the Christmas fifty years ago when I set off with five of my young central African students in an ancient Ford 2-ton pickup on a trip designed to show them parts of their country about which they knew nothing. At night we slept out under the stars, but a day or two before Christmas, we arrived at a "castle" named Shiwangandu.

And what, you may well ask, was a castle doing out there in the wilds of central Africa? Well, it had been built there by an ingenious and enterprising English aristocrat. His name was Sir Stewart Gore-Browne. He came from the very heart of the English aristocracy and even wore that hallmark of the perfect English gentleman, which is a monocle. And in case some of the younger members of the congregation don't know what a monocle is, let me explain. It is really one-half of a pair of glasses. It's just one lens, and you hold it in the eye by pure faith. If you tried to wear a monocle, you'd find it would keep falling out. But if you were an English aristocrat, it wouldn't fall out because you'd have been born with a monocle in your eye, so you know how to hold it in.

43

In a word, Sir Stewart had every reason to be conceited. He was highborn, and he was wealthy, and he had a castle. And he was influential and he was important, and he had a monocle. And one might have thought that when I arrived at his castle door, he would have made me feel about six inches high. And as to the five Africans who were with me, well, he could have made them, if he had been characteristic of many of the white settlers there, feel like five little pieces of dirt.

But, you know, in fact, as we went up those great front steps of his castle, sweaty and dusty, from our hours of travel in this pickup, he swung open those great doors, and he sort of enveloped us in his great big arms, and he made us just as welcome as though we were six of his own sons.

Of course it was the way that he handled the Africans that dumbfounded me. For the custom in central Africa back in those days was for the blacks to go to the rear door of the white man's house, but he had them come in through the front door. The custom back then was for the blacks to sleep in a shed that they called a "kaya," down at the end of the yard. Ah, but he gave them bedrooms that were identical to my own. And the custom back then was to ignore the Africans' hygienic or sanitary needs. If they wanted to wash, they could wash in the river, and if they needed a bathroom, they could go out in the bush. But Sir Stewart provided for the toilet needs of the Africans exactly as he provided for mine.

Then when we sat down to eat, it goes without saying that in no colour-bar country do whites and blacks eat together at the same table. But they did in Sir

44

Stewart's castle, and the same butler that waited on me and brought me my food, waited on them.

Friends, I think I have had very few Christmases that were more radiant and light-filled than that one. That splendid man might well wear a monocle. If ever a man had a "single" eye, it was he – in the truly biblical sense: a view of people undistorted by pride and conceit, or any desire to use them to his personal advantage. And the light that thereby flooded his personality and his attitudes just seemed to illuminate that whole great house and that vast estate of which he was the owner.

"Ah," says the Lord Jesus, "you Christians, if your eye is generous, why, your whole body, your whole life, is going to be full of light."

WEST WINDOW OF GLOUCESTER CATHEDRAL (JOHN 9)

I remember as a teenager cycling with two or three friends from the London area across the south of England to the Welsh border. The trip took us through the ancient city of Gloucester, and one of the teachers in our high school had told us on no account to miss seeing the great west window of Gloucester Cathedral. So on arrival we propped our bicycles rather unceremoniously against the wall of the cathedral, and walked round the outside of the place to see this famous west window.

The afternoon sun was beating down on it, and it was as black as soot. It had not been cleaned, it would seem, since the reign of Henry VIII or earlier. We were totally unimpressed, and could not figure out why our teacher went into such ecstasies about it. However, we decided that before leaving we would take a look inside the cathedral, so we marched in through the north door and were no sooner inside the place than our heads turned in unison towards the west window, which was now a blaze of magnificent colour and exquisite design.

What had happened? No one had cleaned windows. Nobody had replaced the jet-black glass with that stunning display of colour of every hue. No, it was simply that we had simply changed our position. Instead of being outsiders, we were now insiders. As a result the sun, which had been merely shining on the window, was now shining through the window, and penetrating our very heart and soul.

There were some people who got no further than seeing Jesus from the outside, and their comment was, "He's only the carpenter's son. He's just our next-door neighbour." But a fisherman named Peter looked at him and said, "You are the Christ, the Son of the Living God." And a man named Thomas looked at him and said, "You are my Lord and my God."

$1, NEW OR OLD = 100 CENTS
(JOHN 1:1)

If I held up a brand-new dollar bill, how many cents would it be worth? Answer, 100. If I then held up a much used, very crumpled and decidedly dirty old bill, provided it was still recognizably a dollar bill, how many cents would it be worth? Answer, 100 – right? And even if we could go to the Smithsonian and take a look at the very first dollar bill ever issued – the original manuscript, as a theologian would call it – how much would that have been worth when it was in circulation? Answer, 100 cents, no more, no less.

So I do not think we have to worry about the great, historic Standard English versions of the Bible. We refer to them as being infallible and inerrant. By derivation, infallible means that you will get no wrong ideas about God from the Bible, and inerrant that you will get no bum steers on how He wants you to live from it either.

BEDRIDDEN LADY IN FLINT, MI (JUBAL)

Some years ago I was preaching in a church in Wayne, MI. At the close of the service, the pastor told me that every Sunday, after the service was over, he went to visit an elderly lady who had been bedridden for many years. He would leave with her a tape of the morning service, give her a short outline of his message, chat with her and pray with her, and then get on his way home. He asked me if I would like to go with him, and I said I would love to do so.

On arrival we found the lady, as always, in bed. Frankly, I do not remember whether her condition allowed her to be taken out of the house from time to time, but I do know that this one room where we found her was where she spent at least most of her waking hours, and all of her sleeping ones. The wallpaper in her room was arresting. It consisted of hundreds of pictures, cut out from Christian magazines mostly, glued to all the walls in the room except the one directly behind her. Every inch of wall on these three sides was covered with these pictures—pictures of missionaries, pastors, evangelists, Christian friends, and any others that the Lord laid on her heart for prayer.

She asked me if I recognized any of them. I said I recognized Billy Graham and one or two of the missionaries.

"Look over there," she said.

I did so, and immediately saw my own face staring back at me.

"Where did you get that?" I asked.

"Out of the magazine your mission sends me," she said. "That picture was in the issue they published right after you'd been appointed director of the mission, and as soon as I saw it I said, 'Huh, there's a young man that will really need praying for!'"

And since then she had prayed for me every time her eye caught my picture. Indeed she spent all her waking hours praying for the several hundred people she had glued to those three walls.

PBI GRAD IN GARAGE
(METHUSELAH)

There was a young graduate of Prairie Bible Institute (PBI) named George who did all the dirty work on heavy trucks, but the other guys got the bonuses. When the graduate reported this to his wife who was scraping by to maintain the home on a limited budget, she became very angry and told him in no uncertain terms that, "You should go and tell the boss."

But, the boss was in Bermuda. When it looked like a resolution, therefore, might be slow in coming, he chanced upon his principal, Mr. L E Maxwell, walking down the street and shared the same story with him.

LE Maxwell asked George, "Do you mean to tell me that they've been cheating you, robbing you of what is yours, and treating you shamefully and unjustly?"

"Yes," replied George.

"And you've just taken it lying down, without complaining?"

"Yes," replied George again.

"Oh, my dear brother," L E Maxwell exclaimed, enveloping George in a big hug, "it's a long time since I met a man as blessed of God as you are. You're getting treated just like the Lord was treated. And you are reacting just like the Lord reacted – being led like a lamb to the slaughter and opening not your mouth. Stick with it George. Blessed are the persecuted—theirs is the Kingdom of Heaven. I am so thrilled I bumped into you today, into someone who's reaching down to the depths with God, and finding his feet touch bottom."

ITALIAN GIRL AND STATUE

Seventy years ago in London, we small boys did not like being taken on shopping trips with small girls. The problem was that the girls would stop and peer into every window of every store they went by for no better reason than to adjust their hair, each strand of which had to be in a certain position in relation to their ears, eyes, mouth, etc., if their beauty was to make a favourable impression on passersby. Of course we small boys all agreed that, if the girls had looked at the reflection of their faces instead of their hair, they would have realized it was all wasted effort anyway.

However, years later I was told the story of a very poor teenage girl in the city of Rome, who, as she walked along the streets begging, stopped at least once a day in front of one of the statues of the goddess Venus. She did this because she was captivated by the beauty of the goddess's hair. As she stared up at the statue, quite unconsciously she started running her fingers through her own dishevelled hair to make it look like that of the goddess. Then she started to adjust her ragged clothes to look like those of Venus. She even started washing her face, until one day (as you will probably have guessed) a handsome young nobleman was smitten by the beauty, not of the statue, but of the girl who was gazing at it. Of course they both lived happily ever after.

My friends, "we all (and I am quoting a verse from 2 Corinthians 3:18) may behold the beauty of the Lord, and thereby be changed into God's likeness from one degree of glory to another" through the working of the Lord's Spirit within us. That's why says David in Psalm 27:4, "there's only one thing I really want from the LORD, and that is that I might gaze upon His beauty all the days of my life."

SALVATION ARMY GIRL
AS PURE AFTER AS BEFORE
(LOT)

The man who led me to the Lord, Tom Rees, had a friend who was a major in the Salvation Army. This major had one of their supporters visiting with him one evening at about 8 o'clock, just as the workers were leaving to spend the night in some of the foulest parts of the Cities of London and Westminster. The friend could not help noticing that one of the girls he sent out seemed unusually radiant and beautiful, with a clear-textured skin and a look of cleanness and purity of soul that almost took his breath away for the moment.

He could not help turning to his friend, the major, and saying, "Major, are you really sending that young woman out onto the Thames Embankment, to spend the night there with drunkards and criminals and perverts – the very scum of the city of London? I really do not think it is right. She is too pure for an assignment like that."

The major looked at his friend for a moment, and then said, "Harry, I deeply appreciate your concern for that young worker. But I just wish you could see her at

6 o'clock tomorrow morning when she comes back after her night-long stint in all that filth and squalor and sin. She'll be just as pure when she comes back as she was when she went out."

GEORGE CARSON

Only once in my life have I served as pastor of a church, and it was an experience that got off to a very interesting start. The man I was following was a personal friend, and since I had never before been a pastor, and had had no professional training for the job, he kindly agreed to stay around for a week after I arrived, just in case I ran into things I did not know how to handle.

On the day before he left he warned me of one difficulty I might face.

"A week ago," he said, "a man walked into this office and pointed a gun at me and told me he was going to shoot me."

I asked him why, and he said it was because he had ruined his business. The man's business was owning and operating one of these monstrous great "semi" trucks and running it between upstate NY and NC. He would drive it down with a legitimate cargo, but drive it back full of cigarettes on which he deliberately avoided paying NY state tax. He made far more money on the return trip than on the outward one, and was in fact doing exceedingly well out of it. His wife did all the secretarial and bookkeeping work associated with his enterprise, but then, through the ministry of my soon-to-depart predecessor, she came to know Christ as her Saviour and became a brand new woman overnight, as you might say.

She told her husband she was sorry, but she could no longer participate in his illegal, indeed criminal, business – which, of course effectively brought the business to a standstill, unless her husband could find someone as crooked as himself to take the job over. It was at this point that he walked into the pastor's office and told him he was going to shoot him for ruining his business by persuading his wife to choose to follow Christ. With the Lord's help, the pastor talked him out of actually pulling the trigger, but he left the office vowing he would come back in a week, "and that," said the pastor, "is tomorrow, when you will be sitting in this seat, not me."

And the man came as he said he would, though I was relieved to see that this time he had no gun. And he said nothing about his business or his wife.

He said, "You believe in prayer, don't you?"

I said I did.

"Then pray for me now," he demanded. "Tell God I need to off-load my alcohol problem. I have had two drunk driving convictions already, and next time I'll lose my license, and that means I go broke. So pray and tell God I need to get the better of my alcohol problem."

Well, of course, I had to tell him that if he started letting God interfere in his life, God wouldn't stop with his liquor problem; He would go on deal with his whole sin problem.

"He will change you inside out, George," I said, "He will do the same for you as he has done for your wife."

And at that moment, he made his choice. He stopped halting between two opinions. For him it was no longer to be God or Baal. He opted for Baal, and died an alcoholic two years later. The Lord did not reject him. He rejected the Lord.

BILL ELLIS' CONVERSION

Let me tell you about Bill Ellis. I met him when I was a teenager, when our Senior High leader took four of us youthful Episcopalians to a small town in the west of England to conduct an evangelistic mission. When we arrived, our leader hit on the bright idea of going to the local Episcopal rector and asking him who the worst man in the village was, so that we could visit him and invite him to our meetings.

The rector was obviously dubious about our whole enterprise, but nevertheless volunteered the information that the worst man in his parish was the man who had that morning cut his lawn and then stolen his lawn mower, by name Bill Ellis. He made it clear that stealing lawn mowers was the least of Bill's sins, and that he was constantly in and out of prison for theft, but worse yet was a brazen drunkard who beat his wife, and severely mistreated his bedraggled children.

That was clearly our man, so we went off and found Bill. He was not interested in attending our meetings, so our youth group leader offered him a bribe of five English Shillings if he would come. Let me say that this is not standard practice among British evangelists, but this time it worked.

That very first night a semi-intoxicated Bill Ellis sat in the front row, dozed through most of the meeting, but woke up in time to collect his five shillings at the end, and then walked out without a word. The next night, to our surprise, Bill returned, and again sat in the front row, this time sober and wide awake. And best of all, he turned down our offer of another five Shillings. The third night he came back again, washed and shaven, sat once again in the front row, and at the invitation walked forward the short distance to the communion rail, and weeping his eyes out, he dropped to his knees to receive Christ.

And as he did so, God did all sorts of things for him: He forgave him! He released him from inbred sinfulness! He gave him a brand new start in life – the life of a now loving husband and caring father, the life of a man who attracted others to Jesus, and the life of a man, who so far from ever going back to jail for theft, became the city treasurer.

Now that, my friend, is being born again! It's accepting God's free offer of new life in Christ.

TOM REES, DISCIPLER

Certainly, no man was ever a better friend to me than the one that led me to Christ as a 13-year-old. He was our parish youth worker. He must have led at least 100 of us boys to Christ in the two or three years he was with us. I have no doubt that we would long since have drifted away from the Lord, as teenage converts not uncommonly do, if he had not shared with us unstintingly his time and knowledge and encouragement and his youthful maturity in the things of God.

He was, in fact, only four or five years older than we were, but God used him to teach us how to study the Word, and how to pray, both silently and out loud, and how to conduct meetings and give a message.

Some of the things we learned from him we later ditched, and so, in actual fact, did he. For example, we gave up as impolitic the strategy of standing on a warm Sunday evening under the open window of the headmaster of the 500-year-old boys' preparatory school we all attended, and crying out articulately in unison, so that both he and his wife could hear, the words of Jesus as given in the Gospel of Saint Matthew chapter 23, verse 33, "You brood of vipers, how shall YOU escape the damnation of hell?"

But we retained infinitely more than we discarded of Tom's wholesome and practical Biblical insights, to our great and lasting profit, and over the past sixty years that group of youthful Timothys has been expending itself all around the earth in every conceivable phase of Gospel ministry. And I found out years later that he faithfully remembered us. He had a loose-leaf prayer diary the size of a bookkeeper's ledger, and each one of us had a page in it, on which was our picture, and the details of how we had come to Christ, and of the specific things in our lives he felt needed praying for in a special way.

AFRICAN HUNTER'S FIGHT WITH LEOPARD

One day an African who had been badly mauled by a leopard was brought to our mission station. He was a hunter, and while passing through a short stretch of 6-foot-high grass, he had been jumped on by a leopard which got him firmly in his jaws. Hardly knowing what he was doing, he grabbed his hunting knife with his one free hand, and struck blindly. The blade severed the leopard's jugular artery, and after a few moments the great animal lay dead with the hunter still in its jaws.

Fortunately, he had friends waiting for him at the river, and when he didn't show up, they set off through the grass to find him. And when they found him, of course they nearly flipped, for there he was, moaning and groaning, alive but unconscious, in the mouth of this dead leopard.

To cut a long story short, they finally managed to get him out and bought him to our mission station, more dead than alive. The one nurse we had bathed and sterilized his wounds, and bandaged him up. For five days he hovered between life and death.

In due course, he began to recover and the nurse figured she would soon be able to talk to him about Jesus.

But then, a very typical thing happened. His relatives came in the middle of the night and whisked him off home. We saw no more of him until the great annual Bible conference when he showed up, fully healed and smiling from ear to ear. He was the first to stand up at the final testimony meeting and he said something like this:

"You all know how six months ago I was eaten by a leopard and died (in his language, the word "die" is the same as for "being unconscious"). And you know how the nurse brought me back to life. And I asked the other patients why she did so much for us and treated us like we were her children, and why her face always shone with kindness and joy, and they said 'It's because of her God.' And I said, 'Who's he?' And one of them said, 'It's Jesus.'"

"Then Jesus is going to be my God," he said. My friend, the Jesus who became his saviour and Lord and God was the Jesus who had shone like a bright light in the selfless face of that missionary nurse. Much like Paul's vision was of Jesus exalted in the glories of heaven, the African's vision was of Jesus alive in the loving ministrations of a missionary.

DUKE OF WINDSOR
AND TOM REES

King Edward VIII had to give up the crown in 1936 after reigning for only ten months, because he insisted on marrying a twice-divorced lady from Baltimore, MD, named Mrs. Simpson. As king, he was automatically Head of the Church of England, and the Prime Minister agreed with the Archbishops that it was not fitting for the head of the church to be married to a twice-divorced lady from Baltimore, MD.

So he abdicated. He was given the title of Duke of Windsor, and finally settled with his twice-divorced wife somewhere in France. The two of them lived the traditional empty lives of aristocratic socialites who have nothing to do, and far too much money to do it with.

One day, my friend Tom Rees, who had led me to the Lord in 1931, received a long-distance call from France, and the caller identified himself as the Duke of Windsor.

"Mr. Rees," he said, "my wife and I have been reading your recent book, and have been most interested in the stories you tell about people who have, as you call it, found new life in Christ. If we sent our plane up for you, would you be willing to visit us here and tell us more about this new life?"

A few days later Tom flew down and spent most of a day with them. They shared their loneliness and sense of uselessness with him. They told him of their deep bitterness because the Royal Family in England had completely ostracized them, forbidding Mrs. Simpson, or the Duchess as she now was, ever to set foot inside any of the royal castles.

And in the simplest of terms Tom told these two famous but utterly empty people about New Life they could have in Christ, and the very uncomplicated procedure by which that Life might be received.

But when they heard words like "sin" and "repentance" and "confession," and found they were part of the procedure, they visibly lost interest.

And Tom flew back to England, knowing they had rejected the Lord's offer to fill the emptiness that long years of sinful living had created in each of them.

God had in fact created that emptiness in them. But nine years later, when they died, they left no evidence that they had in any way sought to "apprehend the width and length and depth and height of the love of Christ which passes knowledge," and thus be "filled with all the fullness of God," the fullness of that Christ in whom "dwells all the fullness of the Godhead bodily."

They settled for the emptiness, and refused the fullness.

THE HOLLYWOOD ACTRESS WITH THE EPISTLE TO THE ROMANS

It seems to me that these days the world is divided into two unequal halves, one where things like faucets and light switches usually work, and the other where they usually do not, as my wife and I found in Istanbul, where turning on the faucets in bathrooms and kitchens only produced water from 7 to 8 in the morning and during the corresponding hour in the evening.

But there's one thing that always works, and it works all over the world, and it's the Gospel of our Lord Jesus Christ. On my one and only visit to Hollywood, California, about fifty years ago, my host arranged for a stunningly beautiful actress to show me around one of the big film studios. She carried a large book under her arm, which she accidentally dropped. I picked it up, and noticed that it was a commentary on the Epistle to the Romans. She must have seen the amazement on my face, and gave a soft chuckle and said, "Let me tell you about it."

Hers was a fairly conventional Hollywood story. She had arrived in Hollywood at seventeen, had her first child at eighteen, got married at nineteen, divorced at twenty-one. Her daughter, now fourteen, was heavily into drugs, and very much dependent on contraceptives. In fact the two of them, mother and daughter, rarely saw one another.

Said the actress, "My own godlessness never worried me, but when I saw my daughter following me into a life of depravity, I decided I would shoot her and then shoot myself. And on my way to do these two things, I met a friend who asked me to go with her to a meeting for actresses at the Hollywood Presbyterian Church. I was in such a daze that I went, and a man spoke on 'Things that only Jesus can do for you.' As soon as he had finished I went straight up to him and said, 'Sir, how can I get Jesus to do those things for me? I need him to do all of them.' And he said, 'Let's just kneel right here and ask Him.' Jesus did exactly what I asked, and a lot more."

Her story ended with her telling me that her daughter, having spent the first fourteen years of her life following her bad example, lost no time in following her new example. They were shortly leaving Hollywood to go back to Baltimore, to enjoy all the blessings Jesus brings into a life where he is permitted entrance. As I Kings 8:56 puts it, "Let's praise the LORD. He gives deliverance to people just as he promised. Not one word of all His good promises fail which he has given through his servants."

The Gospel works! The gospel works! The actress experienced the transforming power of Jesus, and so can you!

HECTOR MACMILLAN
THE RIGHT TO LIFE AND
LIBERTY?

When the Congo (now Zaire) gained its Independence from Belgium there was a huge struggle for power which resulted in a Civil War with tribal massacres, bloodshed and murder on the widest scale. However, much of the violence was carried out by armed thugs. One such group came to the home of missionary, Hector Macmillan, living in the bush.

When Hector was summoned by Simba guerillas out of his missionary dwelling in Zaire, and knew that he had no option but to walk towards them as they stood with their rifles pointed at him, he did not insist that God honor his right to life.

He simply walked towards the men, and, as his wife and children watched out of the window, the shots rang out, sending his body to the ground and his immortal soul to glory.

His Charter of Rights came from Scripture, and thus, when threatened and reviled, with total assurance, he relinquished his right to life, and "committed himself to Him who judges righteously". Thus miraculously his wife and children were spared for further years of life and ministry. One of his sons and family is now working in Kenya sharing the gospel.

Dr. Helen Roseveare, a British physician working in the Congo, was made captive by those same Simba guerillas, pinned to the ground, and ruthlessly raped. Likewise, she did not insist on any God-given right to life. Instead she settled rather for the blessedness promised to those who are persecuted for righteousness sake.

These folk were Christians who, in the words of Col. 3:10ff, "put off the old self, with its self-centeredness, and have put on the new self, which God, its creator, is constantly renewing in His own likeness".

IMPRISONED CHINA MISSIONARY BEGGING FOR FOOD

One of the many missionary classics produced by OMF (Overseas Missionary Fellowship, formerly China Inland Mission) is a booklet by Mabel Williamson entitled "Have we no Rights?" In it, she outlines those normal, justifiable and elementary rights which she had always taken for granted, but which she found she had quite often to forego if she was to be an effective missionary for Jesus Christ. One, for example, was the Right to a Normal Standard of Living. She found that, to have maintained the standard of living of even a poor American in inland China back in the 1930s would have removed her so far from those totally destitute Chinese peasants that she would have had no meaningful spiritual contact with them whatsoever.

One of her fellow missionaries was later jailed by the Communists when they came to power, and, like all prisoners, including Chinese, she had to buy or beg for food through her prison bars, as none was provided by the prison. She soon used up all the other money she had, and then began bartering her two rings and her wristwatch, then sundry items of clothing. Finally she had nothing left to barter with, and it became a matter of begging or starving. So she begged, and thereby stayed alive, and later gave this testimony:

"When I had things of my own to offer the Chinese in addition to Jesus Christ, I led very few of them to Him. My real ministry to them started when I had nothing to offer them other than Jesus Christ, and then hundreds came to know Him."

WIDOW AT DUNOON
CONFERENCE

Some years ago, I led a weekend conference in the delightful Scottish town of Dunoon, on the bonnie banks of the Firth of Clyde. It was a friendly and responsive group – all except for one lady, who came late to each meeting and left early. After the last session on the Monday morning, she came up to me and apologized for being uncommunicative and unsociable.

She said, "A year or two ago my husband died of a heart attack, and I have never gotten over it. He died while shaving, and his razor is still on the bathroom floor where he dropped it. The papers on his desk are still where he left them. I have not touched one of them. His automobile is still in the garage exactly where he left it last time he used it, and his ocean-going yacht lies rotting in the water. His clothes hang untouched in his closet. I have been totally overcome with grief. But I want you to know," she said, "that over this weekend, even though I have missed out on so much, the Lord has totally released me."

Though I cannot remember the exact words in which she described to me how God had worked in her heart, it was along some such lines as these:

"I have come to see," she said, "that though I have a God-given Right to Mourn, I also have a God-given Responsibility not to become Morbid. I had the Right to Grieve and shed Tears, but no right at all to make everyone else as miserable as I was. And," she said, "it has gone a lot further than that. The large sums of money my husband left are all now mine by Right. But over this weekend I have realized that that Right is not to be compared with the Responsibility I now have to make these funds count for the Glory of God. And," she said, "let me tell you another thing God has taught me. When I came here on Friday, I thought I had the right to shelter myself and cut myself off from people – yes, even from cheerful, friendly people such as we have had here this weekend. I feared lest their happiness would reopen the wound of my own unhappiness. Now I see my Responsibility to give myself to people in fullness of true Christian fellowship and friendship, for it could well be that some of them have sorrows and griefs that go deeper than my own."

ZEUS AND PROMETHEUS

The Greeks called their chief god Zeus. In the days before mankind possessed fire, so the story goes, Zeus lost his temper, when one of his subordinate deities, Prometheus, stole fire from Zeus' personal storehouse, and shared its warmth and cheer with mankind. In his rage at this kindly act, Zeus chained Prometheus to a rock in the middle of the Adriatic Sea, to be tortured with heat and thirst by day, and with the cold by night. For good measure, he sent a vulture to tear out Prometheus' liver, which always grew back again, only to be torn out again and again. And that, if you please, is a concept of deity worked out, not by some barbaric and ignorant tribe of headhunters living in the Stone Age, but by the most cultured, sophisticated and refined people of the ancient world, the Greeks.

JEB STUART MCGRUDER

One of those imprisoned as a result of the Watergate scandal was one of President Nixon's top aides named Jeb Stuart McGruder. As a result of his disastrous experiences, wherein, with his reputation ruined, his job lost, his political power base destroyed, and his whole life in a shambles, like his friend and colleague Chuck Colson, he came into a true personal knowledge of Jesus Christ as his Saviour.

After his accelerated release from prison by Judge John Sirica, he was quizzed on television by three aggressive and cynical newsmen, one of whom asked him rather sarcastically why a nice guy like him would ever have indulged in a dirty, criminal conspiracy like Watergate.

Jeb's answer was almost crushingly simple. It was, he said, because he had allowed himself to be controlled by personal and political ambition rather than by sound moral values. Notice that word "controlled." His whole problem, he told the newsmen, was that he was under the wrong control.

I do not blame Jeb McGruder one bit for not speaking in more specifically Gospel terms to those journalists. Oh yes, he could have told them it was all because Jesus Christ had then had no control over his life whatsoever. He had been ruled and dominated by his own ego, by his ambitions, and his lust for power, and by his relentless pursuit of success and fame. But now, he could have told them, he had been "delivered from the power of darkness and translated into the Kingdom of God's dear son" (Colossians 1:13). To have said all that would have been to cast his newfound pearls before swine.

You would have thought, if you had been watching that television interview, that it was the three newsmen, with their supercilious, disbelieving faces, who had just come out of jail, not Jeb Stuart McGruder. One look at him, and you could see that his life, and his whole personality had become a domain over which Jesus now exercised unquestioned authority.

I do not doubt that he had prayed the Lord's Prayer a thousand times before his conversion, but now as he prayed, "Thy Kingdom come," he found that God took him at his word and answered his prayer. Christ first entered his life as Saviour and sin bearer, and then, with Jeb's willing and eager consent, He took over sovereign control of his life. The Kingdom of God was now "within him," that kingdom which, as the Apostle Paul tells us consists of "righteousness and peace and joy in the Holy Spirit" (Romans 14:17).

GREATER THAN OUR HEARTS
THE SEVENOAKS TEENAGER
DRIVER

Back when I was in high school, one of my Christian buddies was driving his mother somewhere and had a tragic accident. His mother, who had been sitting right beside him, was killed while he himself was unhurt. He was judged to be at fault.

I lost touch with him long ago, but the last I saw him, he was a troubled young man. He was a committed Christian, and had no doubt of God's forgiveness. But he just could not forgive himself.

Says this verse in I John, "If our heart condemns us, God is greater than our heart." And that means that we, who are so infinitely smaller, have no business to go on condemning ourselves for what God, who is so infinitely greater, has forgiven us. If we want to be forgiven, says the Lord's Prayer, we must be forgiving – yes, forgiving even of ourselves in times of our deepest grief if need be.

EAGLET AMONGST TURKEYS

In his book, *The Promise*, Tony Evans tells a mythical story—a parable really—of an eagle that built its nest in a tree on a turkey farm and laid an egg. The egg somehow got knocked out of the nest and fell among the turkeys. The turkeys went ahead and hatched it along with their own. The eaglet hatched, looked around, and saw all these turkeys and came to the logical but false assumption: he was a turkey, even though he didn't look like the other turkeys.

So he began to walk and talk like what he thought he was—a turkey. But one day, a majestic eagle flew over the turkey farm. The eaglet looked up and saw the eagle, and something stirred within him. He felt like he and the eagle were related somehow, but he figured, "But he's up there, and I'm down here."

So he would have forgotten about it except that the great, majestic eagle swooped down from above and asked him, "What are you doing here?"

"I'm just hanging out with my family, the turkeys," he said.

"What makes you think you are a turkey?" said the eagle.

"Well, I was born with the turkeys. I was raised with the turkeys. I eat with them. I sleep with them. I feel like one. I act like one."

The eagle replied, "You have been sadly misled. Stretch out those wings!"

The eaglet stretched out its wings.

"Now flap those wings!"

So the eaglet flapped its wings, and began to rise.

"Flap them harder," the eagle said.

And as the eaglet did what he was told to do by the Big Bird from above, he rose higher and higher.

The big eagle said, "Now follow me," and he took off with the eaglet right behind him.

One of the turkeys looked up and saw the eaglet flying away, and said, "Where do you think you are going?"

The eaglet looked back and said "Going? I am going to be what I was created to be, you turkey!"

Tony Evans concludes, "A lot of us spend our whole lives hanging out with the turkeys, when we might be soaring with the eagles."

YOUNG SOLDIER AND BIBLE
WITH WHITE COVER

Some years ago a story circulated of a young man who went off at the outbreak of World War II to join the British Army. His parents had never been churchgoing people, and the young man himself had been openly contemptuous of those who professed faith in Christ. But a well-meaning country preacher told the boy's mother that on no account should she let him go off to war without a Bible. And it had to be one with a white cover, and the boy had to carry it next to his heart.

It seems that the preacher had once read a story of a soldier in World War I who had been saved from death when an enemy bullet embedded itself in his white-covered Bible instead of in his body. So the mother gave her boy a white-covered Bible. Well, that Bible was an idol. It was not a graven image, but it was something invested by that preacher and by the young man's mother with a mystical and magical power it did not possess.

They were trusting in paper and ink where they should have been trusting in the Lord. An unopened, unused, unread, and unobeyed Bible is not going to assure anyone of God's protection. And any Protestant who thinks it will had better give up smiling at those of his Catholic neighbours who have little religious images on the dashboards of their automobiles to help them avoid accidents. A $10 Bible in the shirt pocket will not free anyone from the need to repent from sin, or to trust in Jesus Christ for his salvation, or to follow Him as His disciple.

WILLIE NICHOLSON AND
BLANKETY-BLANK DRUM

There was once a fiery Irish evangelist named Willie Nicholson, who had been converted from a life so degraded that blasphemy was one of its refinements, not one of its vices. He was so accustomed to using foul language that, for quite a while after he was converted, profanities would even sometimes creep into his evangelistic sermons. On one occasion he told his audience that, the night after he became a Christian, he had been playing the big bass drum in a band.

And "Friends," he said, "I was so happy that night that I could have put my deletable expletive foot right through that deletable expletive drum."

But Willie Nicholson did not go on speaking in that uncouth way. As might be expected, he learned a great deal about holiness of life and holiness of speech as he matured in Christ. He also developed a magnificent command of the English language. Almost completely uneducated though he was, he became an avid reader of good literature. Naturally, he also immersed himself in the old King James Version of the Bible, which was then the only English Bible in use, and the result was that before long he had no need to resort to filthy expletives. He could be infinitely more emphatic in pure English. And please don't ask me where in the Bible there is anything about cultivating the use of good, clean English. In all probability, the answer is Nowhere.

But try it anyway. There is nothing in the Bible about giving up cigarette smoking either, but try that too. Both things will improve your breath.

JAKE MAGGENHEIMER

Let me tell you about my friend Jake. He retired at age sixty from one of the vice-presidencies of the Chase Manhattan Bank, having worked for that organization for nearly forty years, with the one idea in mind of retiring to Florida at age sixty. He wanted to spend the rest of his life fishing and playing golf. So, he retired at age sixty, and settled down to enjoy this treasure he had laid up for those forty long years, and began fishing and playing golf for sixteen hours a day.

But after only a few months, the sheer boredom of doing nothing but playing golf and catching fish pretty well drove him round the bend. So he talked the thing over with one of his fellow retirees, and they came to the conclusion that their real problem was that they had somehow short-changed themselves on religion. Jake was a Jew who had not once darkened the door of a synagogue, and his friend was a Roman Catholic whose last attendance at mass was on his wedding day. So they decided they would start going to church.

Of course, they did not know one church from another, so they just went into the first one they came to. And of all places it was the Presbyterian Church pastored by Dr. James Kennedy. They hardly understood a word of what was said, but on the Monday morning Dr. Kennedy paid a personal call on Jake, and those of you involved in Evangelism Explosion will not be surprised to learn that during that visit, Jake was soundly converted to Christ, and his whole life marvellously salvaged from total uselessness to immense usefulness as he shared his faith in Jesus Christ with literally hundreds in the years that followed. He found out just in time that for forty years he had hoarded for himself a treasure that it took moths and rust only five weeks to destroy. His one regret was that he now only had his retirement years during which to lay up treasure in heaven.

SIR JOHN LAING

When I was involved in educational work in Africa, a year or two after I first arrived there, a proposal was made for the establishing of what would have become Zambia's first Liberal Arts College. The proposal, let me say, finally came to nothing. But while it was still on the drawing board, it had the backing of some English businessmen who were interested in financing it. It was my job to go and see the leader of this group and discuss the project with him.

Now he was a man who had built, during World War II, almost all the giant air bases in Britain, which the US Air Force used in the later stages of that war. Moreover it was reckoned that 50% of all Britain's major highways were being built by his company. And in the immediate post war years, he did not just build houses, he built whole towns. All this was without his vast enterprises overseas. And as a result, he became one of England's three wealthiest men. And this was the man I was going to see.

I will be frank: I was a bit nervous. I had a mental picture of this successful business tycoon, with bushy eyebrows, and a piercing stare, and a lashing tongue, and of course an ability to ask unanswerable questions and slash you down the middle the moment you began to stammer an answer. This was a rich man that I was going to meet, and I was prepared for the worst.

But, you know, that man turned out to be just about as much like Jesus as any man I have ever met. I hope this does not sound blasphemous, but that's exactly how it was. I can remember now how he came out of his house to meet me and slipped his arm into mine and called me by my first name, I can remember how he had me completely at ease within ten seconds, and how we chatted together about the Lord and His goodness, and how we rejoiced at the good things that God was doing for us in Africa. And then, as we reached the front door of his house, which incidentally, was neither a mansion nor a palace, but merely one of the better homes in a subdivision of North West London which he had himself built. I just could not believe that an Englishman that wealthy would open his front door himself.

When all is said and done, even minor British aristocrats have uniformed servants to open their front doors for them, or at least they did back in those days. But no, he opened his own front door, and his wife was waiting there and gave him a welcoming kiss; and while we talked business, she went out to brew a pot of tea, very much like my own mother would have done. By the time I left that house and was on the subway heading back to my home, I had lost all sense of spending an hour with a man who had money enough to buy half the British Isles. I was living in the glow of the graciousness and gentleness of a man who walked humbly with his God, and who had no other concern in life but to let God make him a source of blessing and health to others.

DOUG PERCY'S CALL
AT 10.10 A.M.

I remember once being asked to address the student body of the college which my wife attended in Toronto. I agreed to speak at 10 o'clock on a certain morning. At 10:10 that same morning I was still seated at my office desk, and the telephone rang. It was the dean of the college calling.

"How are you?" he enquired in a friendly tone.

"Fine," I replied, "just fine."

"Are you going to be busy for the next half hour?" he asked.

"No, I don't think so," I said.

"Well, why not come on up here," he said, in not quite as friendly a tone as before. "We have had the whole student body sitting here waiting for you since 10 o'clock!"

That sort of thing really makes a person feel like a bent nickel. The only worse thing is when a preacher forgets to turn up for a wedding or a funeral. All the excuses in the world never make up for a lapse of memory like that.

But that is the way we human beings are, isn't it? We forget our wives' birthdays. We forget we have promised to take the kids swimming. We forget names and faces. We forget our privileges and opportunities. We forget our responsibilities and our obligations. We forget the vows we made in marriage, and sometimes it would seem that we even forget the one to whom we made those vows. We forget the things that are seen, the things of this world, but especially do we forget the things that are not seen, the things of God.

GRANNIE AT OXFORD CURBSIDE

At age eighty-four, my maternal grandmother journeyed to the University of Oxford to see the vice-chancellor of that ancient institution confer on me some degree or another that I had accidentally picked up that year. She was, in the current idiom, a honey.

She was full of laughter, and full of love. Her eyes twinkled. She had neither teeth nor dentures, so that when she closed her mouth, her chin touched her nose. She was less than five feet high: Scottish, poor, and nearly perfect. And she was absurdly proud of her grandchildren. The occasion, now years distant, is still vivid to me. It involved me in a resplendent academic procession in brilliant sunshine down the widest of the Oxford streets. The degree I was awarded on that occasion required me to wear a splendidly colourful hood of which I was childishly proud.

My grandmother stood in the sunshine on that Oxford curb side as the procession went by, oblivious to the chancellors, proctors, honorary doctors and others in their resplendent regalia, clearly convinced that the whole thing had been put on to honour me. So far as she was concerned, the University of Oxford was doing itself a favour in securing my consent to accept one of its degrees!

Improper though it was, I gave her a little wave as I passed her by. She discreetly raised her tiny hand in response, but the real acknowledgment was the glow all over her lovely old face. As I looked into my grandmother's face, I knew one thing for certain: no sense of obligation had brought her there. No one had told her she had to come. She was there because of her love for me, her delight in seeing me acknowledged and honoured, and her happiness in spending the day with people who thought well of me.

DAD'S 7-DAY-A-WEEK NURSES AND THE SABBATH!

My 98-year-old father, after a long and healthy life, had to be admitted into a nursing home as a result of an accident, which left him unconscious and helpless. He was in fact in a coma for eight months. The nursing staff attended him seven days a week, doing everything necessary for his comfort and well-being. But the Fourth Commandment says, "Six days shalt thou labour and do all thy work. The seventh day is the Sabbath of the Lord thy God. In it thou shalt not do any work."

Supposing then that one day the nursing staff had confronted me, as a Bible-believing preacher, and said, "Your father will be cared for only six days a week. The Fourth Commandment forbids us to do more. On the seventh day, please look after him yourself or find some Sabbath-breaking nurses who will come in and suction his tracheotomy, give him his tube feedings and do all the other things we normally do."

In such a circumstance what would I have done?

I hope that the first thing I would have done would have been to assure those nurses that God has indeed left ten eternal and immutable guidelines for holy living, namely the Ten Commandments, and that they were right in saying that only acts which fall within those guidelines are permissible to the Christian. I trust however that I would have gone on to point them to the 6th chapter of Luke, where Jesus was accused by the Pharisees of breaking the Sabbath, because He was planning to heal a man on that day. In response, Jesus asked them a question: "Is it lawful on the Sabbath to do good, or to do evil? To save life, or destroy it?"

And I hope that, in a kindly way, I would have asked those nurses the same question, somehow persuading them that the rightness or wrongness of deeds done on the Sabbath can only be determined by reference to the Lord of the Sabbath, the Son of Man, namely Jesus. What He would have done in the same circumstance is what we should do. I might also have referred them to Paul's words in I Corinthians 3:6, "The letter kills. It is the Spirit who gives life."

DR. BARNARD AND FIRST
HEART TRANSPLANT

One of the earliest heart transplant patients, whose life was prolonged by Dr. Christiaan Barnard of Cape Town, lived two years after his surgery. Eighteen months after leaving the hospital, a reporter asked him what his main ambition was, now that he had been given this almost miraculous new lease on life.

His reported reply was, "My main purpose in life at this moment is to persuade Dr. Barnard to let me have a glass of beer once again, whenever I want one."

Millions of dollars went into buildings, equipment and personnel needed for this type of surgery, and out of all that came a man with a newly activated thirst for beer. One really wonders if the surgery was really worthwhile. Life indeed is precious; but the value of that sort of living is not very obvious.

WINKIE AND THE STOLEN COOKIES

Proverbs 25:16 warns us that, "a false witness is like a bludgeon or cudgel, and like a sword and a sharp arrow." It can inflict deadly damage – worst of all to someone's good name and honourable reputation. Some of us had to learn this the hard way in Africa.

On one occasion, a missionary lady made a big batch of cookies each day for some special mid-week function we had on our station. On the first day, she went off to a meeting, and on her return the cookies had totally disappeared from the tray on which they had been left to cool.

She had noticed, as she approached her house, that her houseboy, an African of course, was just leaving the kitchen. So in considerable agitation she called him back and asked him if he had eaten her cookies, clearly implying by her tone of voice that she knew perfectly well that he had. He of course denied it, though he knew that his denial would not convince the lady one little bit.

You see, it was commonplace amongst us white people in Africa back in those days. Even amongst us missionaries, I regret to say, that Africans as a group were thieves and liars. The next day she baked another batch, left them to cool, and once again went off to her meeting. But this time upon her return, it was her dog, not her houseboy, that she saw leaving the kitchen, with cookie crumbs all over its face. Once again the cookie tray was empty. This offered a logical explanation for the event of the previous day, so she went to the servants' compound to call for the houseboy, so that she could tell him that he was now cleared of suspicion.

But word came back that he had left for home. He had quit his job. And as far as I know, none of us ever saw him again. And the thing that still gnaws in my mind is whether the same thing happened to him as happened to thousands of other young Africans at this point in the history of central Africa, when there was increasing cynicism about white people, and disillusionment with them. Many of these young Africans, under the political banner of independence, turned to violence and theft, and it could be that this houseboy was one day arrested by the police, and put in jail. It's even possible that a prison chaplain visited him and asked him what had made a nice kid like him do a thing like that. I know what his answer would have been, and it would have been simple:

"A white missionary said I stole her cookies. From then on I was known as a thief. She changed her mind, but no one else changed theirs, so I could not get a job. So I just became what she said I was, a thief."

ALAN STAINES AND MY CONVERSION

I used to be a rather objectionable little boy aged twelve, who went to school each day with a number of other rather objectionable little 12-year-old boys in my hometown. Most of us were good friends, but one of them was my sworn enemy. I have often tried to remember why, but cannot think of one good reason, for he was no more and no less objectionable in the general sense than I was. The whole thing came to a head when our parish church, founded incidentally in the year 10 hundred and something and rebuilt in 14 hundred and something, appointed a new youth pastor, who started leading the boys in our town to Christ in an unbelievable manner.

One of the first to come under his influence, believe it or not, was this sworn enemy of mine. Disaster finally struck when, one day, he crossed the road. Let me explain that there were no school busses in those days as we all walked to school. The mutually hostile relationship between the two of us had made it obvious to us both that, if he walked on one side of the road, I should walk on the other, and vice versa. But this particular morning, as I say, he purposely and deliberately, I would even say brazenly, crossed to my side.

Trouble was clearly brewing, or so I thought, until he spoke to me in a normal, friendly sort of voice, and chatted easily with me until we reached school. I had to admit it, that, from that point on, the look on his face was changed, the tone of his voice, and – well, every last thing about him was changed. When he finally started to share with me what had happened to him at that new boys' Bible class, I had to believe him.

Why? Simply because his witness was true. It was true in content – Jesus Christ had obviously done a fantastic job on him; and it was true in motive – he had no further interest in demolishing me, as he would have had if he had been a false witness. He wanted to see me fall in behind Jesus Christ, just as he had done. And, by God's grace, I lost no time in doing so. Unlike myself, he did not live to a ripe old age, but died in his late fifties. But his faithful and true witness to that One who is Himself THE Faithful and True Witness (Revelation 3:14) has brought blessing, benefits and joys into my life which I cannot count: years of happy service for the Lord on three continents, a beloved Christian wife and family, and the assurance that, when God's moment arrives, I shall receive that ultimate benefit of that true witness, namely an eternal place in the very presence of God.

HOG CHASES HOG

Covetousness destroys contentment. One preacher tells how, as a boy, he used to feed the hogs on his parents' farm. He would carry out a basket that contained at least a hundred ears of corn, and pour them all on the ground. The supply was ample for the needs of all. But there was always one stupid hog that would grab an ear of corn, and run up the hillside with the cob in its mouth as if running for its life. Then a second and even more stupid hog would at once abandon the great pile of cobs still on the ground, and pursue his fleeing fellow. This it would do, said the preacher, with squeals and whines as bitter as a spanked child's tears. That was all it got out of being covetous in the midst of plenty.

COVETING THE PASTOR'S STUDY IN DAMASCUS, OR

A good many years ago I was invited to preach in the city of Portland, Oregon. On arrival I was given an instant reminder of the fact that being a pastor offers no automatic immunity against the temptation to break the tenth commandment, and to give way to xovetousness. For, you see, as I stepped into the pastor's study in the church where I was to be preaching, I had, as it were, my moment of truth relative to this tenth commandment.

For his study was more than twice the size of my own back there in upstate New York. It was carpeted wall to wall with material so thick that I could have slept on it. The paneling of the room was solid walnut, as was his enormous desk, and the place was equipped with every conceivable electronic gadget on the market. What finally reduced me to spiritual ruin was to find that one of the doors in this palatial, book-lined study of his led to a complex comprising not only a private bathroom, complete with shower, but a private kitchen and sitting room. If that preacher got to be wearied, either by the members of his congregation or by his own sermons, he could go in there and take a quiet nap!

For a passing moment my mind flew back to what now seemed the mere hole in the wall that at that time served me for an office. Of course, it lasted only for a moment. I did not really have the slightest desire to have a couch to recline on or a private bathroom complete with shower. But it was just enough time for the Lord to remind me that being a preacher assured me of no automatic immunity against covetousness.

SAMSON MAKEPESHI'S JACKET
AND HIS UNCLE

Let me tell you about a jacket I gave to a young African on my staff over forty years ago. Back then, it was one of the dreams of an African who lived out in the bush to possess at least one garment of the sort worn by the white man. So when I handed him that jacket, which incidentally fit him like a glove, his eyes opened wide and beamed with pure delight. He now had the thing that they all desired – one might say they really coveted – more than anything in the world: a garment from England. The following Sunday I met him coming to church with his uncle. This was the man who had raised him, since he was an orphan, and for whom he had great love and indeed admiration.

But lo and behold, the uncle was wearing the jacket, and the young man, my colleague, was still dressed in his same old bits and pieces. I confess, my friends, my indignation was considerable, and I would have addressed some stern words to that covetous old so-and-so, if my young colleague had not turned to me with joy in his face that glowed brighter even than when I had given him the jacket.

"Oh, Bwana," he said, "I am so excited that the jacket you gave me fits my dear uncle. Thank you for giving it to me."

Friends, I can see it now, though I could not see it then. Jesus had transformed that wonderful young Christian's coveting from the sinful sort, coveting merely because of greed, into the sanctified sort, coveting above all else to be as non-self-seeking as Jesus—that Jesus who had said, "Give to him who asks of you, and from him that would borrow of you, do not turn away." And even at eighteen years of age, out there in the African bush, he had found that Jesus was right: There is more blessing in giving that receiving.

BERT RUDGE'S FLUID DRIVE

Not to be forgotten is the day when we bush babies in central Africa got our first glimpse of an automobile equipped with automatic shift: no gear stick, no clutch, just step on the gas and go. We couldn't believe it. Well, in due course our visitor drove off in his automated air cushion, on down the exceedingly rough bush road towards the next mission station, 140 miles to the southeast. But he never made it to the next mission station. He never made it anywhere indeed. About fifty miles down the road, that seemingly miraculous transmission gave out on him. Late that afternoon an African on a bicycle arrived from the scene of the breakdown with a note imploring us to come down and help him get him out of his predicament.

But all that we had on our mission station was an antique Model A Ford pick-up, an extremely bent Model A at that, considerably battered and liberally begrimed with African mud. We eventually drew up alongside this gleaming Chrysler Imperial. It seemed almost like sacrilege to attach a chain from our Model A to this Chrysler behind us. But attach it we did, and we pulled the Chrysler all the way back fifty miles to the mission station: $30,000 worth of helplessness being salvaged by 100 bucks worth of trustworthiness.

Just be reminded then, my dear friends, that it is what is on the inside that counts. Our politicians can all too easily fool us with their flashy exteriors, but neither they nor we can fool God, not even for a split second. There's a famous verse in the OT (I Samuel 16:7) which says that "Man looks at the outward appearance, but the LORD looks at the heart."

Why do we not all ask the Lord to look into our hearts, and take whatever action on us He sees is necessary?

THE LONG AND THE
SHORT OF IT

There is no difference," says Romans 3:23, "all have sinned and come short of the glory of God." "That's ridiculous," someone might say. "Is the Bible saying that I am as wicked as Adolf Hitler who burned six million Jews, or that guy who murdered thirteen little girls and buried their corpses in his backyard?" Well, probably not. The word Paul used for "sinned" in that verse means "missed the mark" or "came short of one's goal."

It's like those two guys who went to enlist in the famous British Grenadier Guards – the ones who stand outside Buckingham palace, and are distinguished by their "busbies," those fur hats about eighteen inches high, which come so far down over their eyes that you wonder how on earth they can see where they are going.

Well, back in the old days you had to be six feet tall to join the Grenadiers. And they say that one day, two men entered the recruiting office to join up. One was tall and one was short.

And the tall one sneered at the short one, "Don't be stupid," he said, "you've got to be a tall man like me to the join the guards."

The short one, who was a cheerful little guy, said, "OK. I thought I'd just let them measure me anyway."

So in he went, and in ten seconds he was out again, having been found to be 4 ft 11 inches in height, in other words, too short. The tall man went in, and in ten seconds he also was out again, with a big scowl on his face. He had likewise been measured and found to be 5 ft 11 inches in height, in other words, too short. There was no difference. Oh yes, one was taller than the other, but they were both too short for the Guards.

So, friends, let's all stop comparing ourselves with other people, and start comparing ourselves to Jesus Christ. It won't take us long then to understand what Romans 3:23 means when it says that we have all "come short." That is why you will hear it said time and time again here in this church, that everyone, everyone without exception, needs Jesus – as their Saviour, Sin Bearer and Lord.

LITTLE MARY AND THE GRAPES

Every Sunday, when I was six or seven years of age, my sweet Scottish grandmother would read me a story from her book of sacred tear-jerkers, most of them about a poor wee Scottish lassie named Mary and her widowed, and deathly sick mother. The one I remember best was about that sad day when little Mary's mother, who had been so sick that she had not been able to eat for days, suddenly told little Mary that she thought she could eat a few grapes.

But, you see, in those days grapes were way beyond the budget of the poor in Scotland, but so what! Off went little Mary to see if she could buy some with the two pennies, which constituted the total wealth of her and her mother. My grandmother and I of course both knew the end of the story so by now we were both crying our eyes out, because we knew that the man at the local store would not even let ragged little Mary inside the place, let alone sell her grapes.

So she set off back home, but as she passed the big gates of the Duke's castle, right inside was a greenhouse full of grapes. Little Mary put her nose to the glass and stared at them longingly, but you see the Duke's beautiful young daughter was inside the greenhouse and

117

came straight out and scared the daylights out of little Mary by asking her what she wanted. With tears pouring down her face, and of course down my face and my grandmother's face as well, she told the beautiful young lady her sad story.

At which point the beautiful young lady went back into the greenhouse, cut the biggest, juiciest bunch of grapes in there, brought them out and gave them to little Mary, gently pushing away the two pennies she was offering for them.

"No, Mary," she said, "keep your two pennies. You see, you are far too poor to buy from my father, and my father is far too rich to sell to you."

TRUTH OR FICTION?

When one lives out in the middle of nowhere in a place where one has almost no visitors, those who do unexpectedly drop by can be quite unusually interesting.

Few called in on us on our central African mission station. How would they ever get there – the nearest railroad depot was 240 miles away and the road between it and us was either a joke or a catastrophe, depending on how you view such things.

Imagine our surprise then, when one day a truck did pull in unannounced. The friendly occupants were a film crew who had come out on behalf of some Hollywood outfit or another to shoot scenes of "African life as it really is." They wanted us to have the Africans dress themselves up in leopard skins, carry spears and shields and to have pieces of ivory protruding from their noses and lips. When we told them the Africans in our area did not go in for any of these items, they said, "No problem, we have plenty of stuff in the truck." They dressed everyone up the way they thought "real Africans" should look. They then took the film back to show to audiences back in Britain, explaining that no one back home would pay money to watch a film on Africa if it didn't make everything look fierce, savage and murderous.

Dressing one's self up just to make a big impression! I guess we have all done it at times. Like they say, "You can fool some of the people some of the time, but you can't fool all of the people all of the time." Here in Britain the headlines have recently all been taken up with the death (many suspect suicide) of the biggest of our newspaper publishers. He was reputed to be worth billions of dollars, with a private jet and helicopter, a luxurious ocean-going yacht, and all the other bits and pieces which establish a man as "successful." Then at 5 o'clock one morning he disappeared over the side of his boat naked, and was not missed until his body was found floating in the water some hours later. It has turned out since that he was, in fact, not the richest man in the world, but one of the poorest. He owed the banks billions.

Now, I guess, he's standing before God, naked, penniless, shamed, guilty. Now he has nothing with which to camouflage himself, no way to convince the Almighty he is not really the sort of man he so obviously was. If only someone could have told him that God sent Jesus into the world precisely in order to remove our need of such camouflage, by redeeming us, cleansing us, transforming us, and finally presenting us in heaven "without spot or wrinkle or any such thing."

RESEMBLANCE

Have you ever been told by someone that you remind them of somebody else? We all look like someone or another, I guess. We have recently added a new grandchild to our family, and before he was a week old everyone was expressing an opinion on who he looked like.

"Isn't he like his daddy!"

"Oh no, I think he is exactly like his mommy!"

Fortunately for the little guy, no one suggested he looked like me! A year or two ago, however, I found out that I did look like someone. I was preaching in a fairly big church in New York City and after the service a lady came up to me in tears. Hoping I could be of help to her, I suggested she share with me what particular point in my message had moved her that morning.

"Oh, it's nothing to do with your message," she replied, "it's just that up there in the pulpit you looked exactly like my father. He was a preacher too, and died last year."

What I look like had inspired her more than what I said, which wasn't surprising as I'm not all that great a preacher.

It made me think of something which had happened to the son of a man I knew. He was an M.D. and was working as a missionary doctor amongst one of the Indian tribes in Central America. He was driving his jeep across the sub-desert back towards his hospital when he thought he heard a cry. He stopped, thinking perhaps an animal had gotten caught in a trap, and walked towards where the wailing sound was coming from. He found the trap all right, but it was not an animal that was caught in it, but an old Indian lady who, he learned later, had been sent out into the desert by her tribe to die. That apparently was their custom.

He opened up the trap, gave her a shot to relieve her pain, then carried her gently to the jeep and took her back to the hospital. He personally took care of getting her comfortably settled between the clean, white sheets in the ward, and each day he'd go in to see her. He spoke her language fluently, so he was able to reassure her and even cheer her up quite a bit, though she had little to look forward to.

Since it was a mission hospital, there was naturally a pastor on the staff who tried to tell each of the patients about Jesus. Some of them were interested and some were not – that's how it is everywhere in the world, isn't it? But even though he went to the bedside of the old lady at least twice a day, he couldn't get to first base with her. He didn't speak the language all that well and she just did not seem to understand one word of what he was trying to tell her.

Finally the day came for the old lady to leave the hospital and the pastor got desperate. "I've got to make her understand," he said to himself. So in he went for his last visit with her, and with the simplest words he could find, slowly and clearly, he told her again about Jesus. He'd just about given up when the ward door opened and the doctor's cheery face appeared. He gave the old lady a wave, but seeing the pastor was busy talking to her, he apologized for intruding and left, saying that he would come back a little later. As the door shut, light seemed to come into her bleary old eyes.

She looked up at the pastor and said, "Is this Jesus you're talking about like the doctor?"

"Yes," said the pastor. "He's a lot like the doctor: kind, caring, comes to help us when we are really hurting" and so on.

"All right," she said, "if Jesus is like the doctor, I want Him."

We all look like someone, don't we? What a different world it would be if more of us looked like Jesus!

I NEED TO KNOW WHY

I seem to remember there was some scientist or philosopher some years ago who predicted that, with the rapid progress of human knowledge (going to the moon, computer technology, etc.), it would not be long before man would understand everything and have an answer to every question.

I hope it's true, because I've got one question no one seems to have an answer to. Here's how it came about: some years after my arrival in central Africa in the early 1940s, a colleague and I took a trip along a "road" which had been cleared through the bush by those who plotted the boundary between the then Belgian Congo and the then British colony of Northern Rhodesia. It was much overgrown and very rough, and hardly anyone ever used it.

We made the trip in a half-ton Model A Ford truck. (If anyone ever gets to heaven by good works it will be Henry Ford for his Model T and Model A.) About halfway between nowhere and nowhere on this road, and about 120 miles from anywhere, one of the rear springs collapsed, and the rear end sank right down onto the tires. A thing called a kingpin, which held the spring to the frame, had fallen out.

125

We were immobilized in lion country! The only answer was to hoist up the rear end and insert a pole as a temporary replacement for the spring. The pole was no problem out there in the bush, but where could we get some Africans to help us hold up the rear end? We knew we had passed no villages for at least forty miles, so we strode forward after praying a quick prayer that we'd find some soon.

But before we found the Africans, we found something else. Down there on a bare spot on this overgrown road in the middle of the central African bush was a king-pin. Yes sir, I said a kingpin. The rest of the story is easy. We found some Africans. They lifted up the rear end while my colleague inserted the kingpin (it fit!), and off we went towards our destination 120 miles ahead.

So what I need now is for one of these scientists and philosophers to tell me how things like that happen. We knew there was a trader who occasionally used that road, so it was conceivable that a kingpin had dropped out of his tool box. However we were never able to ascertain that he had done so recently; and even if he had, WHY, out of all the countless bits and pieces a man like that would carry in his tool box, did it have to be not only a king-pin, but a king-pin which fit our little half-ton truck, that dropped out on that rarely travelled bush road in the middle of nowhere?

Just a coincidence, many people would say. But that's not an explanation. For "coincidence" specifically means something you can't explain. So my mind goes back to that quick little prayer that we prayed. God, our loving heavenly father, clearly had something to do with that kingpin being there.

SMILE! GOD LOVES YOU!

A year or two ago I went to Yugoslavia for conferences in various of the churches there. We were excited to find them flourishing even though communism had not yet been overthrown.

One result of my long connection with Africa is that a great many of my sermon illustrations are drawn from that wonderful continent. So when the conferences were over, the leaders of the churches approached me. Their imaginations had been fired by my many references to Africa, and they had come to realize how completely ignorant they were of the place and what missionaries were doing out there. They were keen to learn more and in some way or another to get involved. They asked if there was any chance I could come back to Yugoslavia before too long and bring a real, live African with me!

Neither they nor I saw any real possibility of that happening, but in point of fact, a year or so later it did: An African pastor friend of mine, who had been invited to take part in a conference in the States, gladly arranged his flights so that he could make a week-long stopover in Yugoslavia. I met him at the airport in Zagreb and we went straight to one of the churches. The building was packed with people in their best Sunday clothes which, in the case of the men, meant thick dark suits and shirts with very stiff white collars. They all looked most uncomfortable. In fact, they looked as though they had assembled for a funeral rather than the happy experience of meeting a real African Christian for the first time. Following the Baptist tradition in Yugoslavia, the men sat on one side of the church and the women on the other, dressed in black. All were solemnly staring on the ground. They obviously felt it was irreverent to look cheerful in church!

In due course, the African pastor went up into the pulpit with the interpreter and found himself looking out on this seemingly glum group of people all staring down at the floor. He couldn't figure out why no one looked up and smiled at him. I guess the situation struck him as a bit comical, for a great beaming smile came on his face as he stood there in the pulpit waiting for them to look up at him.

Finally a couple of people looked up, wondering, I guess, when he was going to start his talk. They saw this cheerful black face with its beaming smile, and almost at once their own solemn countenances started to thaw and they smiled back. Before long everyone else was looking up and undergoing the same transformation. Soon, it was as though bright warm sunshine had flooded the building and everybody was now bright-eyed, smiling and eagerly waiting to hear what he had to say. That meeting was one of the most joyous and relaxed meetings I have ever been in. That African has been a hero out there ever since.

It all came from a smile – that look of joy and wholesomeness in the African's face. It made me wonder how often my face had that sort of effect on people. It's more than possible that at times I have soured people up just by looking sour myself.

GETTING IT STRAIGHT

Most of the courses I took in college were of the egghead variety. They resulted in me becoming mildly "intellectual," but left me completely useless in all things practical.

This proved a disadvantage when I was given my first missionary assignment in central Africa. It was to build a house. Building houses was something not included in my egghead courses, so what was I to do?

One thing I was definitely not going to do was to admit to anyone out there, white or black, that I'd never in my life built a house and didn't have the first idea how to go about it. You can't admit that sort of thing when you've accumulated more college degrees than all your colleagues put together.

My problem proved to have a simple solution. All around me, I reasoned, were Africans who had been building African houses for years and years. Clearly all I needed to do was to co-opt a few of them and we'd get the job done in no time. So I approached three likely looking young men and mentioned casually that I was going to build a house for the African preacher.

"Care to give me a hand?" I said.

"We'd love to," they said.

131

I then asked them how Africans went about building a house – what was the first thing they did. They said that first of all they measured out the footings.

"Great!" I said, "that's just the way we do it back home. Go right ahead." So that took care of the footings.

Soon we were ready to start building. I asked them how Africans went about that part of the work. They told me that they always built the corners first.

"Can you believe it?" I replied. "That's just how we do it back home. Let's go!"

I was hopeful, of course, that just as they had gone ahead and done the footings without help from me, they would now go ahead and build the corners without help from me. But it was not to be. One of them came up with the suggestion that, since there were four corners and four of us, I should build corner number one and they would build the other three.

Now up until that point in my life, the only brick I remember ever holding in my hand was one I had picked up to throw at a cat which was meowing in the middle of the night under my bedroom window. Never in my life had I built with bricks. But once again I found that the problem had a simple solution. I just built my corner by sneaking glances at the three Africans to see how they were doing theirs, and then did mine the same way, with one exception.

The exception was that they were fussing around with pieces of string with little stones tied to them, and using them as primitive plumb lines. This slowed them down considerably. I found I could make much better speed by keeping my eye on a tall, straight tree that was growing near my corner. I tried to look very professional as I closed one eye, squinted at the time, and made my

132

corner go up dead straight – as dead straight as the tree, that is.

Before the end of the day the four corners were all completed and it looked as though the next day we would finish the walls and start the roof. At 6 o'clock the next morning we were back on the job, and I found myself facing a new and quite unexpected problem. Three of the corners were still standing firm and erect, but the fourth, the one I had built, was a heap of rubble!

Now Africans are the most wonderful people. Those guys didn't say a thing to make me look small, though of course by now they knew full well that I knew nothing at all about building houses. Very tactfully they explained to me why a seemingly straight tree is no substitute for an unquestionably straight plumb line. The fact that it might be far straighter than all the other trees around did not mean that it was absolutely straight, certainly not straight enough to be relied on for measuring the uprightness of things like the corners of new houses.

I'd gone to Africa to educate Africans. This was where they began to educate me. I learned the absolute necessity of using a plumb line if you are going to be sure that your building is straight and won't collapse in a heap.

Plumb-lines must still have been in my mind when I next preached in the church on the mission station, for I spoke on an incident in the life of an Old Testament prophet named Amos who said he had had a vision. "I saw the Lord," he said, "standing on a wall, with a plumb-line in His hand."

"He was measuring His people," I explained, "and making it clear to them that they were not as straight and upright as they proudly professed to be."

"One day," I went on, "I guess we are all going to find ourselves being measured by God's plumb-line. It won't help us much to tell God that we were a whole lot better than most people. True, we didn't go to church very often, but we were a lot better than most of those who did, etc., etc. That sort of self-measurement will at that point in time prove totally irrelevant. It's God's plumb-line that will reveal the truth."

"But cheer up," I concluded. "A plumb-line isn't the only tool a builder holds in his hand. His main implement is the trowel. He doesn't just check measurements: he builds houses, and if necessary rebuilds them. And what a building you have when God builds it!

Give Him a chance to build your life," I concluded, "and it will not be long before others will be asking (behind your back of course) how on earth a guy like you manages to stand so tall and live so uprightly in a world as crooked as this one."

FINDING THE RIGHT WORD

Some words don't mean now what they used to mean. "Conversation," for example, now means having a friendly chat together. Originally it meant "behaviour." A "bum" now means a beggar. It used to mean a buzzing sound, hence "bumble" bee.

One word that surprised me was the word "gossip." The current dictionary defines "gossip" as "spreading tales about someone's private life, often maliciously." But originally it was a combination of two words, "God" and "Sib." "Sib" means your brother or sister – we still use the word "sibling," which means the same. "God-Sib" therefore meant "someone related to you in God," such as the one who sponsored you for baptism, or even the friend who acted as your midwife!

The good old word "gossip" then has gone a long way downhill over the centuries, meaning, as it now does, telling tales about people behind their backs, spreading scandal, and so on. Gossip of the modern sort was what years ago finished off that lady in the Scottish highlands whose tombstone reads:

Beneath this sod, a lump of clay,
Lies Arabella Young,
Who on the twenty fourth of May,

135

Began to hold her tongue.

In her case, being a gossip clearly had nothing to do with being a midwife!

Dr. Charles Swindoll gives the following advice to those wanting to overcome a tendency to engage in unkind gossip.

1. Think first
2. Talk less
3. Start today

To these, I would add:

4. Estimate the damage

Gossip can be devastating. Just yesterday I read in the paper of an 18-year-old girl who passed on to her circle of friends the spicy information that she had had sex with a 50-year-old man. As a result, he was later charged with rape. At the trial, the defence lawyer produced medical evidence that the girl was still a virgin, so the man was cleared. He was not present at the trial and when his attorney went to give him the good news of his acquittal, he found that he had already committed suicide. Gossip can be devastating.

Let me just repeat, for my own benefit as much as yours, the advice of Dr. Charles Swindoll on how to stop gossiping:

THINK FIRST!
TALK LESS!
START TODAY!

GAIN AND LOSS

I don't know how many people used to say during my trips home from Africa, "You must be clever to be able to tell one African from another. They all look alike to me!" The funny thing was that the Africans thought the same – they said all white folks looked alike!

The fact is, of course, that, similar as we humans may look, there are still big differences between us. Take for example the different ways in which people react when things begin to get difficult or painful. Some seem to have the ability to look on the bright side and ride them out, while others collapse in a heap right at the start.

Never will I forget the president of the college I attended years ago in the University of Oxford. Before leaving Oxford to take up a new job, he took his family on a much-needed vacation in Ireland.

One day they went out to sea in a boat, and on return, had to land on a very rocky piece of the Irish shoreline. The only way to do it was for one of them to jump onto the rocks and secure the boat so that the others could get out. So the president himself jumped out, but he slipped on the wet rocks and his right leg was crushed between the rocks and the boat. He was rushed to hospital and was told that his leg had to be amputated.

But he was one of these people who don't collapse in a heap when bad news hits them. He'd been through some very tough spots in the First World War, had been wounded and decorated for bravery. He'd returned to the front as soon as he had recovered from his injuries. No one was surprised therefore when he told the doctor to repair his leg, not take it off. This went on for six months, but then the doctor told him bluntly, "It's amputate or die." So off it came.

Along with many others, I sent him a letter of condolence. It had been a long, hard and apparently useless fight, and he had lost it. His reply was characteristic.

"Thanks for your sympathy," he said, "but quite frankly I don't need it. During these six months of enforced inactivity in hospital, I've been renewing my acquaintance with God. I've been talking to Him about all sorts of things, and you'll never believe the things He has been talking to me about as I have read through the Bible. I can easily do my new job with only one leg, but I know now that I could never have done it without the inner refreshing and renewal I have received while in that hospital bed. "Indeed," he concluded, "I would give my other leg if I could get another dose of blessing like that!"

I knew of course that he was exaggerating. But I got his point. His God was a God who could turn loss into gain, and even make suffering an enrichment. It's not of course that God always does this. But it's worth giving Him a chance, isn't it? For we certainly seem to gain nothing at all by putting on a sour face and acting as though there were no God around to give us a bit of help and encouragement when we need it.

DIFFERENT, BUT HOW DIFFERENT?

I am writing this in a Mayan Indian village 7,000 feet up in the mountains of western Guatemala. Anything less like the places where I usually do my writing, namely the very conventional English town of Sevenoaks, can hardly be imagined.

I wish I had time to describe the Mayan village and its colorful and cheerful inhabitants. I sincerely hope that not too many tourists will find it. The Mayans are too noble and too ancient a people merely to be stared at as relics of a past age or objects of curiosity, simply because they wear quaint and highly colored clothes woven in their own homes, or because their children carry on their backs loads of up to eighty pounds strapped to their foreheads.

What a lot of differences there are between us humans who inhabit this old globe! Yes, and what a lot of astonishing similarities too! I'd never met a Mayan Indian until a week ago, and now they seem like old friends. It was the same when I first arrived in central Africa fifty years ago. My first impression was of the very obvious differences between myself and the Africans.

Their physical appearance, their homes, their food were all different – the latter included such tasty items as flying ants (roasted) and cane rat stew, which incidentally I later came to enjoy very much.

Then their family relationships were different – I would even say richer – than ours. One day one of my African assistants asked me if I would like to accompany him on a visit to his home village. I leaped at the opportunity and shortly after arrival he introduced me to his mother. I congratulated her on her fine son and told her how much I appreciated all the help he gave me. She could, I said, be very proud of him.

Then we went on to meet other members of the family. As a second woman approached us, my African friend said, "Oh, good – here's my mother." I just assumed I'd heard him wrong the first time, and so gave the second lady the same little speech as I'd given the first one.

However, when a little later he introduced me to a third lady, telling me he'd like me to meet his mother, I said, "Now just a minute. How many mothers do you have?"

Without blinking an eyelid he said, "At least six." Later he explained it all to me. His real mother had five sisters. In his tribe they were all regarded as his mothers, and all their children were his brothers and sisters. One good result of this was that there were no orphans in that part of Africa. If a child's actual mother died, he had plenty of others to whom he could go!

But the differences between me and the Africans ran even deeper than that. One lady who visited our school campus quite often had withered hands. I wondered if she had had polio, but was told that her problem was not polio but twins. In her tribe only a woman who was the victim of evil spirits had twins. To get rid of the spirits she had to go to the witch doctor, who put "medicine" in a large pot of water, and then told her to put it on the fire and plunge her hands into it when the water was boiling. Whether she lost the spirits that way, I don't know. She certainly lost the use of her hands.

Differences! That's all I saw at first. But it wasn't too long before the similarities quite eclipsed the differences. I found Africans cried at the same things I cried at, and laughed at the things I laughed at. One day I went off to preach in a remote village way out in the bush, but there was no one there. The people had gone off to plant their corn about four miles away. So I sat down to await their return, and then noticed that one small villager had in fact stayed behind. He was about seven years of age, and was wearing nothing but a string of beads round his middle. He didn't take much notice of me. After all, I wasn't a real "person." How could you be a real person and not be black? He may even have thought that I was some new sort of gorilla. Anyway he had more important things on his mind. He was hungry!

Now it was the time of year when food was scarce, but he knew that there would be a huge bunch of bananas hanging from the roof in the hut where he and his family lived. From the furtive look on his face I could tell that his mom had instructed him to leave those bananas alone, or else! But finally hunger overcame fear and he went into the house, climbed up the centre pole, and took a large, ripe, scrumptious banana.

He came out of the house very cautiously, looking this way and that just in case....! But the coast was clear, so he peeled the banana down to just above the halfway mark, and was about to lift it to his mouth when – PLOD, PLOD, PLOD – could that be his mother arriving home so soon? Quickly the half peeled banana disappeared behind his back and yes, sure enough, there was mom coming straight across towards the house, with his baby sister tied on her back and a large pot of water on her head.

Mothers are mothers, aren't they? It makes no difference whether they are white, black, Indian, Chinese or whatever. If they are mothers, that's what they are – mothers! Which means, amongst other things, they can turn up at the wrong moment! And what's more, they cannot be fooled – one look will tell them if their 7-year-old has stolen a banana or a cookie or some candy, or whatever it is the kid has been told not to take. This African mom didn't need to be told anything. She paused just one brief moment to take the water pot off her head and then advanced on the little culprit.

I won't tell you the end of the story because you can guess it! But as she whacked that little sinner's bare backside, I swear I could feel the whacks my own mom gave me on the same part of my anatomy nearly seventy years ago. That kid may have been black, and I white, but our cartoon humanity was a more fundamental factor than our superficial differences. We humans may be widely different in our lifestyles, but we are remarkably similar in our sins. And that's why somewhere down the line, all of us equally – be we Mayan Indians, African villagers, or anything else, are going to need some forgiveness. Thank God it is always within reach.

LAW AND GRACE:
A JEWISH STORY

There was a poor widow, who had two daughters and a field. She had no sooner gone out to plough her field, than a rabbi came by and quoted Deuteronomy 22:20 at her: "Thou shalt not plough with an ox and an ass together."

Not having a second ox, she left her ploughing, and planted the portion she had already ploughed with seed. Whereupon a second rabbi came by and threw Leviticus 19:19 at her, "Thou shalt not sow thy field with mingled seed."

So she quit sowing and contented herself with the small area she had already sown. But later, when she went to reap her small crop, a third rabbi came by and hurled Leviticus 19:9 at the poor soul. It says, "When thou reapest the harvest of thy land, thou shalt not wholly reap the corners of thy land, neither shalt thou gather the gleanings. Leave them for the poor and the stranger."

So she did what he said, and went home with a pitifully meager supply of wheat. However, when she began to thresh it, yet another rabbi came by, and his text was Deuteronomy 12:6, "Give me your uplifted offering, your tithe, and then a freewill offering."

So she gave him her uplifted offering and her tithe and the required freewill offering, and this just about cleaned her out. So, fearing that she and her two daughters would starve, she sold her field and bought two sheep, so that they could clothe themselves with their wool and have profit from their young. But as soon as the sheep bore lambs, a priest came by, and using Exodus 13:12 as his pretext, demanded the firstborn for himself.

She handed it over, and later on, when shearing time came, she cut off the wool from the remaining sheep. But another priest saw her at work, and piously uttering Deuteronomy 18:4, he reminded her that "the first of the fleece thou shalt give to the priest."

So she gave him what he demanded, but thought to herself, "I cannot stand up against these thieving rabbis and priests. Before another one comes by, I'll slaughter the sheep and my daughters and I will eat them."

But she was not fast enough. A priest must have been right round the corner, and he immediately advanced upon her with the verse, "Of an ox or a sheep, give to the priest the shoulder and the two cheeks and the stomach." That's Deuteronomy 18:3.

In a last desperate effort to salvage her livelihood, she cried out, "My sheep are Corban, that is to say I have dedicated them to God."

"In that case," said the priest, "I'll take the whole lot, for Numbers 18:14 says, 'Everything devoted to the Lord shall be the priest's.'"

Thus, says the story, the poor woman went home, and sold her house, and walked away to die, with nothing but her two daughters and her tears, having been robbed blind by the custodians of the Commandment which says, "Do not rob anyone."

FOLLOWING THE WRONG MAP

In 1961, the general secretary of the United Nations, Dag Hammarskjold – one of the best and the best known general secretaries the UN ever had – was killed in a plane accident in Africa. What caused the crash was not at first apparent. It was a clear night, there was no storm, and the crash took place in a relatively flat, open field. Terrorism was of course suspected – the Congo was then in a state of civil war, as it still is – but when they went through the wreckage of the plane, they found that the pilot had been following the wrong map.

The crash occurred near the Zambian city of Ndola, 240 miles north of the SIM hospital where our son, Steve, is now serving. But in the wreckage of the plane a map was found opened at the page showing Ndolo – one letter different – a town not too far away, just over the Congolese border. But Ndola is 1,000 feet higher than Ndolo, so the pilot made a tragic miscalculation, and ran the plane into the ground, thinking he was somewhere other than where he really was. He was simply following the wrong map.

PARABLE

Mark 4:34 says that Jesus never said anything to people other than his disciples without illustrating it in some way or another. Mark's Gospel tells us, in fact, that, when speaking to ordinary people like ourselves, he never preached a sermon or delivered a lecture. Instead he always spoke in parables. "Without a parable," says Mark, "he never gave a speech of any sort."

What would Jesus have used as parables today? Probably not things like mustard seeds and a man going from Jerusalem to Jericho. Possibly something to do with the winter Olympics or satellites going into orbit or something of that sort. I don't know. But I do recollect that, the first time I went up the Empire State Building in New York City a great many years ago, I wondered if that wouldn't have provided Jesus with a pretty good idea for parable. I remember as I stood looking over the edge, 1,300 feet up in the air, I was accosted by a man in a peaked cap with a gun in his holster. He was some sort of custodian or security man, and sensing I was a foreigner, he proceeded to give me the history of the building.

"When WE built this place," he said, not mentioning what specific part he had in building the Empire State Building, "the rock WE dug out to make

147

sure we had good foundations weighed more than the whole building weighs." – and by the whole building he meant all 102 floors of it. Clearly the architects and construction people had given primary attention to the foundations.

Well, there's a parable. We clearly live today in a world where foundations have a habit of being neglected.

Occasionally I reread the story of Howard Hughes, the eccentric multi-billionaire who amongst other things owned Trans World Airlines, which he had purchased as a sort of plaything. I look at the pictures of him in the later years of his life, living in total isolation from the whole world, existing on nothing but drugs, suspicious of everyone, loved by no one; and I say to myself, "That man must have based his life on totally wrong premises." I'm sure he meant to end up happy, content and admired. In fact he ended up miserable, shriveled and despised. Those pictures usually made me say a little prayer to this effect, "Dear God, I am quite ready to settle for a great deal less money than that man had if I can end off with lots of good friends, a happy family, a sense of fulfillment, and a situation where those around me are hoping I will live a little longer, not that I had died a lot sooner."

There's no two ways about it, one's foundational convictions are of the highest importance. I suppose this is where Christianity comes very significantly into the picture, for one of its main jobs is to provide a sound basis for living – sound aims and objectives, sound attitudes, sound principles and ideals and so on. And I personally have found that it does so. Preachers usually call it "Building your life on Jesus Christ," or "Committing your life to Jesus Christ," or "Following Jesus Christ." It doesn't matter much what you call it as long as you do something about it. The superstructure of your life will be no sounder than the foundations that you build it on, and I'm pretty certain you'll not find any sounder basis for living than following Christ.

I went from New York City to the west coast of America, and took the opportunity to see a phenomenon called the Grand Canyon of Arizona. It is an immense crack in the face of the earth, a mile deep, ten miles wide, and well over a hundred miles long. Once again I was accosted by a man in a peaked cap with a gun in his holster who, sensing I was foreigner, proceeded to give me some information on the thing.

"Want to know something?" he said. "You could go all the way back to Adam and Eve, and take all the people who've ever been born anywhere in the world since then, and lay them down in this canyon end to end and side by side and in layers, and when they was all in you could just put a lid on the top and you wouldn't know no one was there."

While I was expressing the hope that no one would try such an idea, he was asking me another question. "Do you know what caused it?" he asked.

Not being a geologist, I said No.

"I'll tell you," he said. "That little river down there, the Colorado River done it."

It seems that the river had gone on running across the state of Arizona century after century, and because no one had done anything about it, it just cut that enormous hole on the earth's surface, and finally made it so large and so unmanageable that in order to get to the friends waving to you from the other side only a mile away, you have to drive 240 miles. The Great Divide is of course the line running along the peaks of the Rocky

149

Mountains, but the Grand Canyon is a great divide of another sort. It is, to use a Bible phrase, a Great Gulf Fixed.

Yes, I thought, as I stood there, there's another parable. The Kingdom of Heaven is like unto the Grand Canyon of Arizona. It's like that rather contemptible little Colorado River, which in its turn is like that Something which runs through all our lives. Goodness knows what it really is, perhaps it's just our human natures, but if one does nothing about it and lets it go on without keeping an eye on it, by the time we are thirty or forty, and possibly a lot sooner, it will have made a most immense gap in our lives between ourselves and all that is decent and upright and worthy. We will find, to revert to preacher's language, that God is on one side of life and we are on the other. Willy nilly, without planning or forethought, without being evil or wicked, we shall find ourselves Godless, faithless, and therefore all too often aimless, even possibly hopeless, and in the ultimate analysis, helpless.

Would you pardon me therefore if I make a couple of recommendations? First, if you sense that gap may already have begun to appear between you and God, that you ask Jesus Christ to close it. One of his old titles is Pontifex Maximus, the Supreme Bridge Builder or Closer of the Gap.

And second, like the architects of the Empire State Building, that you give priority consideration to the foundation upon which you are building your life. I can guarantee with very substantial assurance that you will not find a better foundation than Jesus Christ. His life on earth will provide you with an unsurpassable fine pattern. Service to mankind in His Name will provide you with the most fulfilling of all reasons for living. His death will provide with forgiveness for your failures, and His Spirit with a dynamic confidence for the future. Frankly, I cannot fathom why more people do not give Christianity a real honest-to-goodness try.

THE BIG LEAP

At the moment of writing, my wife and I are rushing around getting ourselves ready to leave at the crack of dawn for Switzerland. If you happen to be one those who haven't visited this beautiful little country, remember the (quite fictitious) prayer reputedly offered by one of the Saints: "Lord, please don't take me to heaven until I have first seen Switzerland." It is quite unique even amongst the many very beautiful places there are down here on God's earth.

Every time I go there, various Swiss stories come to my mind. One is of a group of tourists who hired an experienced Swiss guide to take them to the top of one of the Alpine peaks. It was rugged and challenging, but all went well until they came to a crevasse in the ice. When the tourists saw the width and depth of it, they wondered how on earth they would ever have the nerve to cross it. However, the Swiss guide jumped easily to the other side, got himself securely positioned, and then held out his hand to the first member of the party, and said, "Take my hand and jump!" The man did so and landed safely in the snow on the other side, followed by the rest.

All except one lady. She had gone as near as she could to the edge of the crevasse and looked down. There was just no bottom to the thing! And the width of it! And the slippery ice! In terror she had gone right to the back of the line but finally it was her turn to make the jump. Real fear now took hold of her and she said to the guide, "I'm sorry, I just cannot do it."

The guide did not try to persuade her. He simply held out his great weather-beaten hand, and quietly said, "Lady, take a look at that hand. For the past twenty-nine years it has been taking people over this crevasse and it's never let one go yet!"

The lady looked into his eyes, took his hand, and jumped over as thousands had done before.

I don't spend much time fussing about my final end. But I'm mighty glad to know that when I myself am next in line to make the Big Leap, there'll be a Man standing on the other side with a great, strong Hand – a nail-pierced hand – stretched out towards me.

"Put your hand in mine," He'll say. "Not one who in simple faith has put his hand in mine has ever been let go, and you are not going to be the first."

"Peter's Final Big Leap" was on
December 17, 2013.

About Peter Letchford

Peter Letchford was born February 16, 1917 in Sevenoaks, Kent, England to Arthur and Beatrice Letchford. He graduated as one of the two "poor boys" from Sevenoaks School (1935). He studied at Oxford University, matriculating with a BA, BMus, '42, MA '45. While a student, he served in the leadership of the Intervarsity Christian Fellowship.

Upon graduation, Peter answered the call to work with the Africa Evangelical Fellowship (AEF). Along with his colleague Ginger Wright, he was instrumental in establishing the education system in the northwestern part of Northern Rhodesia (now Zambia). Many of his graduates became national leaders at the time of Zambia's independence in 1964. During his subsequent tenure as Canadian Director with AEF in Toronto, Peter met and married Dorothy in 1960.

Peter's career included helping to establish the Graduate School of Missions at Columbia Bible College (now Columbia International University), senior pastor at Loudonville Community Church (Albany, NY), General Director of The Hildenborough

155

Evangelistic Trust (England), and as pastoral associate at First Presbyterian Church (Augusta, GA).

Peter was an excellent communicator using stories from his young life through to his later life. With this skill he was able to take a subject that needed clarifying by using incidents from his life to illustrate a point he was making. Many of these were told with a sense of humor and wit. Whether in table conversations or in sermons, this gift kept his audiences spellbound.

Peter was known for his commitment to God, his love for his wife, delight in his children, belief in others, wisdom, intellectual curiosity, compassion, and humor.

97171799R00087

Made in the USA
Columbia, SC
12 June 2018